Research Strategies

Research Strategies

Finding your Way through the Information Fog

3rd Edition

William B. Badke

iUniverse, Inc.
New York Lincoln Shanghai

Research Strategies
Finding your Way through the Information Fog

iUniverse books may be ordered through booksellers or by contacting:

iUniverse
2021 Pine Lake Road, Suite 100
Lincoln, NE 68512
www.iuniverse.com
1-800-Authors (1-800-288-4677)

NOTE that an online page for additional information and updates is available at: http://www.acts.twu.ca/lbr/updates.htm

ISBN: 978-0-595-47747-0 (pbk)
ISBN: 978-0-595-60504-0 (ebk)

Printed in the United States of America

Acknowledgements

I would like to recognize the strong support and encouragement of my colleagues at Norma Marion Alloway Library, Trinity Western University, Langley, BC, Canada. Your mutual respect and collaborate spirits have made my experiments with information literacy instruction both easier and hopefully more mature. You are all a blessing.

A special thanks to my new comrade in arms, reference librarian Duncan Dixon, who is helping us forge fresh directions in information literacy. He was of great help with a number of the graphics in this book.

And thanks to EBSCO Publishing for permission to use screenshots from their databases.

Contents

8. Learning How to Read for Research 136

Preface

Everyone does research. Some just do it better than others.

This book is definitely for you if you are:

> ➢ a university student whose term papers have been patented as a cure for insomnia;

> ➢ a Dilbert of industry who's been told to do a feasibility study on the expansion potential of ice cream bar sales in Nome, Alaska;

> ➢ a simple honest citizen trying to find the truth behind the advertising so that the next car you buy won't be like your last disaster-mobile, the car that made you *persona non grata* at the automobile association.

Are you ready for your next research project? Really ready? Do you have the skills and strategies to get the job done efficiently and effectively without panic attacks and the need for a long vacation when you're done? Do you have confidence that you can start with a topic about which you know nothing and end with an understanding of it that is neither trite nor superficial? Are you prepared to enjoy the experience? (Yes, I did say "enjoy.")

If the previous paragraph has left you feeling somewhat queasy, this book is for you. Even if you have significant research skills, you can learn better ones if you take the time to read on. You have the privilege of living in the information age, with so many opportunities all around you to find out anything about anything. But faced with a humongous number of Internet sites, not to mention academic and commercial databases of increasing size and complexity, knowing how to navigate through the information fog isn't something you can pick up easily on your own.

Yet you can hardly call yourself educated if you don't know how to handle information systems and do research effectively, not in a world in which most careers are built more on what you can find out than what you already know.

Who am I to try to teach you about research? Just someone who has introduced the strategies in this book to hundreds, nay thousands, of anxious university students, both undergraduate and graduate, over 20+ years, and who likes nothing better than to walk people through the information fog. I am Associate Librarian for Associated Canadian Theological Schools and Information Literacy at Trinity Western University. Being the author of a number of books and scholarly articles myself (see my bio at **http://www.acts.twu.ca/lbr/badke.htm**), you can rest assured I've devoted a lot of my life to *doing* research and not just teaching it. So I understand what you're going through.

One caution: This book is about *informational* research. It won't teach you how to do a science experiment or determine the best way to train a rat how to ride a tiny bicycle (though the research model I am using could apply to both situations). But if you need to identify a problem, and then acquire and use information to address the problem, this book is for you.

Learning how to do research does not have to be painful. It can be fun. Honestly. Personally, research gives me so much pleasure that my family has to kidnap me out of the library whenever they want to go on an outing or buy groceries. You can have the same joy that I have. Read on.

1

Welcome to the Information Fog

At one time we thought we knew what information was. Now we're not so sure. These days we're buried in the stuff, and defining what is and what is not information is getting to be more of a challenge all the time.

Information is supposed to inform. That means it has to be reliable, relevant, current, and so on. There was a time when people believed that, given the right information, we could solve any problem the human race encountered. They thought that the power of reason could be used in a totally objective way to wade through all the relevant data and come up with the right answers, even with the truth. Now we're no longer even sure what the questions are (and we can't remember last Tuesday).

To be sure, we've always known that some of what passes for information can't be trusted. That's why we have law courts to determine the truth of a matter (though the best liar often wins).

We've come to understand over the past hundred years that information is colored with subjectivity: What we know depends on how we interpret what we read and hear. Even the authors of information bring their own biases into the mix. Thus, for good or ill, we are no longer as trusting when it comes to information. It's like buying a Rolex from a man in an alley—it might be a real Rolex coming from somebody down on his luck, but, unless you know Rolexes, you could well be getting a knock-off.

I'd like to take a bit of time to trace the events that have led us to this place. Textbooks, after all, are supposed to lead you on a daunting journey through history and philosophy-of-whatever before they get to the good stuff. But in the case of information, the next few pages really are essential to doing good research, so I'm not going to apologize for them, and you don't have my permission to skip to the next chapter.

1.1 Before There Was Print

Throughout the entire history of humanity, knowledge has been passed down from one generation to another. Before this was done in written form (and in preliterate societies today), speech and demonstration were the source of humanity's information—historical tales told around campfires, children learning about agriculture by doing it with their parents, and so on. These were "traditional societies." I use the word "traditional" not in the sense of 1920s country music and picket fences, but in the sense of knowledge viewed as a *tradition* to pass down from generation to generation, for the very survival of the society.

Here's an example of why these kinds of societies need traditional information: When I lived for a couple of years in Africa, people would point to this plant or that and tell me, "You could eat this." It happened often enough that I finally asked someone why it was so important for me to know what plant I could eat. He explained that during the recently ended civil war, the people had been driven from their city homes into the jungle. They were starving, because no one knew what plants were edible and what were deadly. Their ancestors had carried this knowledge with them, but these city dwellers had stopped passing it on to their children, and the knowledge had died.

So the urbanites, now living in the bush, cooked various plants and fed them to their chickens to see if the chickens would chirp or croak. And gradually they rebuilt their knowledge base. "We have decided," my friend told me, "that we must never again forget what we can eat, so that's why we tell one another what is edible." Their traditions had meant survival to the society. Forget what you can eat in the jungle and you'll have to choose between possibly poisoning yourself and starving.

Clearly, though, traditional information has to be reliable. Thus, in societies that depend on their traditions, knowledge is passed down only by people qualified to do so, and unregulated production of new information is not encouraged. There is an emphasis within traditional societies on memorizing the information that exists rather than using existing information to create new knowledge. The development of new knowledge in such cultures is a deliberate and slow process performed with care and authorized only by experts in the existing tradition. Otherwise, the next plant you eat could well be your last.

1.2 Reading and Writing

The development of *written* language brought a number of changes to the world:

> Knowledge could be preserved in print, thus there was less of a need to pass it on orally (though the oral remained important), let alone a need to memorize huge amounts of information. Memorization continued, to be sure, but you didn't need to know everything, because it was possible to look it up if you had access to written documents.

> Since the knowledge base was more secure, people could pay more attention to discovery, thus hopefully adding to the knowledge base.

> The keepers of knowledge (i.e., the tradition experts) were more elite than they had been in an oral society. Now only people who could read could stay close to the tradition. What is more, there were few copies, because everything had to be transcribed by hand. Thus a small group of people in the society controlled the knowledge base, and these people (recognizing that knowledge is power) generally worked against the forces of discovery (who tend to take the power away from the people who control the knowledge base). As long as access to documents was controlled, most people continued to rely more on oral tradition. The full transition from all oral to mainly written took many centuries.

1.3 The Printing Press

The Chinese actually invented the printing press centuries before the Europeans did (as was the case for many things, including gunpowder), but it was the Europeans who used it to revolutionize the use of information in society. In 1447, Johannes Gensfleisch zur Laden zum Gutenberg (Gutenberg for short) created a moveable type press, a development so revolutionary that the A & E Television Network in 1999 named him #1 in its list of "People of the Millennium." The printing press was such a big deal because:

> From a "preservation of the tradition" standpoint, it meant that multiple copies could be produced, thus making the tradition more secure (previously, it would have taken only one match lit by a careless monk to burn the single manuscript that had everything you needed to know— sort of a medieval hard-drive crash).

> More people could actually get their hands on the knowledge base, thus creating a better-informed society that was not as dependent on oral tradition. The elitism of knowledge was attacked as "holders of

the tradition" found they no longer had an exclusive right to control who saw the knowledge base and who added to it.

> The possibilities of discovery were greatly increased, because so many more people had access to existing knowledge. It was thus much more likely that new knowledge would be built on the foundation of the old.

The multiplication of knowledge in the centuries that followed, along with all the major discoveries that make our lives what they are, owe most of their existence to the printing press. Yet there were pros and cons to this invention. The pros are obvious, the cons not as much. First on the con side, the printing press was only as useful as the population was literate. We are still working on that problem.

Second, a new form of elitism developed, and whether it was good or bad remains a matter of debate. It came from the fact that production of new information depended on two things: bright people to make the discoveries and money to publish their words. The bright people created the elitism of universities and the money people determined what would be published and what would not.

The money issue put a limit on who could get his or her ideas into print. Publishers, wanting to be sure they didn't lose their shirts, added "gatekeeping" processes to their requirements. Gatekeepers ask two key questions: First, is the information worthy to be published? This is a value judgment, usually based on level of scholarship or reliability or entertainment value, but sometimes based on the aims of the publisher or the demands of the marketplace (thus the existence of romance novels). Second, will it sell? Many a worthy manuscript goes into the garbage can simply because the publisher doesn't think there's an audience to sell it to. Alternately, there might be a small audience that has to pay a large amount for each copy published (as with most scholarly books).

Gatekeeping is a good thing when it helps to preserve quality. No one wants our knowledge base to be filled with shoddy stuff that no one can trust (or so the wisdom of commercial publishing would tell us). On the other hand, gatekeeping has been used to censor valuable information, keeping it away from the very people who need it most. This has prevented perfectly good ideas from seeing the light of day, simply because someone viewed those ideas as unacceptable or there wasn't a good market for them. Thus gatekeeping has often tended to maintain the status quo, because new, radical concepts are not as sure to sell as the tried and true.

Certainly, people have always been able to self-publish material that the gatekeepers rejected, but distributing self-published books is a tough game. Would-be buyers often ask, "If this is such a good book, why didn't the commercial publishers want it?" Thus self-published material tends to stay more or less underground.

Along with the printing press has come development of the "subject discipline," allowing people to specialize in particular fields of discovery. The idea of a "discipline," a defined subject area within which discovery is made, has its good points (the main one being the ability to focus narrowly in order to provide more depth of research) and its bad points (the main one being the separation of knowledge into categories that don't talk much with each other). But the fact is that most advancement of knowledge these days is done within disciplines.

What does that mean for people doing research?

> ➢ Each discipline has its own "language" which is more than just its technical words but also involves the ways in which that discipline communicates information. A historian has a different mode of expression than that of a physicist (or an expert in the sex life of nematodes).

> ➢ Each discipline has its own method of doing research. While method, even in the humanities, has some connection with the scientific research process, there are distinct features that make research in English literature different from research in Korean history or in the biology of nematodes.

> ➢ Each discipline has its in-crowd, its elite group of highly regarded scholars. Knowing which writers and which works are most highly regarded is very important to doing research without looking like an outsider.

1.4 Enter the World Wide Web

A revolution as revolutionary as that of Gutenberg has happened within our own generation—the creation of the World Wide Web, a popular subset of the larger Internet. In the short span of time since the early 1990s, the WWW has blown to blow the lid off much that we've known about information since the beginning of time. Why? Because it has pushed aside most of the boundaries that once prevented us from having all the information our knowledge-greedy little eyes would want.

It comes down to one basic fact—*On the WWW, any fool can publish almost anything he or she wants to say, without impediment.* I use the word "fool" on purpose, not to offend anyone, but to demonstrate the full extent of the reality of the WWW. Let me unpack it a bit:

➤ On the WWW, gatekeepers are no longer required. They still exist, and they still have great value, but we can publish without them. Whether or not it's advisable to do so is another issue, but for the first time in human history we can have our say without anybody stopping us. The Internet, for good or ill, is the greatest vehicle for free speech that we have ever known.

➤ We can publish and acquire information at a level never before possible. The Web enables us to have access to so much, in fact, that we can easily be overwhelmed by it. As far as getting our own message out, we have a potential audience that can number in the millions.

➤ What we lose (perhaps) is certainty. If any fool can publish on the WWW (and many of them do), we lose all the normal checks and balances that kept us from being inundated by nonsense. This isn't a new problem, because even with gatekept print material, readers should always be exercising discernment. But we now have the challenge that, for a large portion of Web-based information, no one except the author has done any gatekeeping at all. This is a classic two-edged sword—if any fool can publish on the Net, then we have an amazing resource for freedom of speech and the democratic way of life. The old elitism is gone. But it also means that *we, the readers, have to become the gatekeepers.* This demands that we must enhance our evaluation skills.

Before you accuse me of being overly simple-minded (something I've heard a lot), let me point out that it's not as "either-or" as I may have implied. You see, the WWW is really less a content-provider than a *vehicle* for information, like, for example, the phone system. Thus it is also used by publishers who still carry out rigorous gatekeeping procedures. E-Books and scholarly articles are carried by the same system that provides us with Aunt Bertha's remedy for lumbago. Many of these resources are part of the "hidden" or "invisible" Internet (found behind password gates so that only authorized users can see them), but they have as much of a home on the WWW as your cousin's jumpy YouTube video of river-rafting last summer.

One more feature of the WWW that we need to consider is the function of electronic documents. If a document is in electronic form, is it different from the same document in paper form? At one level we'd have to say "no," because the content is the same regardless of its format. Format is thus irrelevant. Whether I read it in a book or off a screen, the message is the same.

But Marshall McLuhan, the Canadian techno-philosopher, argued that "The medium is the message," meaning that the format we use for communication carries as much of a message as the words themselves. This is certainly true for electronic documents. Electronic documents are not the same as print ones, even if the words are the same, for the following reasons, among others:

> ➤ They can be distributed widely within a very short time period, thus making them far more current than print.

> ➤ They can be easily altered without detection.

> ➤ Copies can look entirely different from one another in font, print size, spacing, color, etc., so electronic documents are more malleable than print.

> ➤ If the document has hyperlinks to other document, the reader docs not have to stay within the document itself. Do the hyperlinks thus become part of a larger "document" that includes the original text as well as the content of the hyperlinked pages?

> ➤ If the document is hyperlinked within its own content (through bookmarks or a web of hyperlinked pages), the reader need not read it in order as is commonly done with a print document. This disrupts the idea of a document as a linear progression of thought and may work against the interpretive guideline that every piece of data must have a context.

Thus an electronic document upsets the very meaning of the word "document." Electronically, a "document" can be viewed from anywhere in the world at the same time via the Internet. It can have its wording and its look changed at will without any sign left behind that there was an earlier version (though the Internet Archive does a good job of preserving old versions of Web sites: **http://www.archive.org/index.php**). It can encompass other documents as well as encourage reading out of order. This may be exciting (for example, we can hyperlink a document so that any possible problem or interest a reader may experience can be answered with the click of a mouse), but it carries dangers as well:

> ➤ The fact that an electronic document can be created and flashed around the world in an instant may also mean that half-blown ideas can be shared as if they were the more well-formulated concepts of a print document.

> ➤ The fact that a document can change both its wording and look without leaving a sign that there was an earlier version can lead to revisionism (rewriting history) of the worst sort.

➢ The ability to hyperlink is also creating a loss of the sense of context. Just as isolated words have no certain meaning unless put in a sentence, data in documents, if not read in context, loses its certainty, and true communication disappears. While the footnotes and endnotes have always created the risk that we would be drawn away from the document we are reading, hyperlinks have the power to pull the reader completely away from the original document.

All of this has scholars wondering how best both to preserve and define "documents" so that electronic data can be at least as stable as print while retaining its hyperlink capabilities.

One approach to preservation of electronic data has been to rethink copyright for electronic documents. Copyright has traditionally controlled who can pass out a document and in what form. It has also protected the text of the document by preventing it from being published in altered form as long as any of the content is the same as the original. One form of the old style elitism is the concept of "licensing" documents, that is, delivering them in such a way that the user can have access only by agreeing to certain conditions imposed by the producer or vendor. If those conditions are violated, the user can be prosecuted for breaching a contract.

Copyright protection does have its place, especially when it is trying to preserve the text and the look of a document, but there are powerful forces out there who are working very hard to end the "tyranny" of copyright and make all information available to anyone who wants it, without cost.

1.5 Information Today—The State of the Art

Let's look at some of the main sources of information today:

1.5.1 Books

Book publishing is continuing, with no hint of a slowdown in the process. While many publishers now provide e-book versions of their print works, most publishing houses still see electronic book publication as a risky business with not much likelihood of making significant cash.

To this point, readers have not been completely thrilled by e-books either. While there are reasonably good libraries of e-books available (Questia, netLibrary, Ebrary), the response to them has been underwhelming. Most people respond to e-books with the question: "Who wants to read a whole book off the screen?" Newer display devices (such as the Sony Reader and Amazon Kindle, both of which use E Ink) are deliberately easy on the eyes and may be the solution to screen-glare.

There are some advantages to e-books, however. They can get information into the hands of more people. As well, the ability to search for content in them using keywords could make them good research tools.

The disadvantages come from eye strain, lots of scrolling through pages, and the potential that searching for keywords could lead to using material out of context.

New initiatives are helping the e-book process. Beyond better reading devices, more publishers are signing on to provide content, and Internet-based projects using digitized books look promising—Project Gutenberg, Google Book, Live Search Books, Amazon A-9, and so on. For a list on ongoing book digitization projects, see Wikipedia: **http://en.wikipedia.org/wiki/List_of_digital_library_projects**.

While most book publishing continues to have a strong gatekeeping component, there is a growing movement, fed by newer "print on demand" technology, which is supporting print book self-publication without the enormous cost and distribution problems that once existed. You can now, for $1000 or less, publish your own book (even having it editorially reviewed) and have it distributed through normal book distribution channels without the need to have 5,000 copies in your basement. Does quality suffer in the process? Possibly, though even without gatekeepers a lot of self-published authors are putting out high quality material that traditional publishers did not consider marketable.

1.5.2 Journals and Magazines

The handwriting is on the wall for paper versions of scholarly journals, though magazines and possibly newspapers still seem to be holding their own in print form. Most scholarly journals now have electronic versions and offer subscribers the option to get a subscription in print or in electronic form. As the popularity of electronic versions grows (and it definitely is growing), more and more journals will begin appearing electronically only.

Why are electronic journals doing so well, while e-books are not?

> ➤ Journal articles are shorter, thus easier to read online.

> ➤ Subscribers often don't read all the articles in a journal issue anyway. If they want to retain certain articles, it is easy to print them from electronic form.

> ➢ Students like the convenience of having articles instantly available rather than having to look for them on the library shelves or (horrors) in microfiche cabinets.

> ➢ Journal databases (more on this later) provide a way to combine searching for relevant articles and actually getting the electronic full text of those articles in a single process.

Popular magazines, though most of them provide web pages and sample articles, have been slower to publish only in electronic form, mainly because people like taking them on the bus or to the beach. Lugging along a computer to read them with (or even downloading them to a hand held device) makes them less convenient. The newspaper world, however, is getting quite a shake-up from the many people who prefer to subscribe online (and read the paper while at their jobs) instead of dealing with messy newsprint. Amazon's Kindle offers the opportunity to read several daily newspapers in eye-friendly e-paper format—electronic but kind to the eyes.

Does all of this electronic publishing diminish quality? Not really. Most scholarly journals continue to use the gatekeeping process of *peer review*, by which submitted manuscripts are evaluated by scholars in the subject discipline in order to determine whether they are worthy to be published. This is a key distinction between a scholarly journal article and what you might find through the average Google search. A Web site on the topic may be as electronic as the journal article on the same topic, but the journal article has been checked out by experts before it ever sees the light of day. Maybe those experts were biased or missed something important (like faked lab results), but on average the peer review process does provide more confidence that the article is reliable than you would have from a Web site on the same topic written by your uncle Fred.

A serious challenge to the availability of scholarly journals has been price. The average annual journal subscription can range from $50 to the cost of a new Toyota Corolla. Only the major universities can afford a full range of journals, thus limiting who can get access. A number of public bodies that fund research have done a double take and said, "Wait a minute. If we fund the research out of public money so that scholars can publish articles (getting paid nothing for doing so) and then publicly funded universities have to pay through the nose for the journals that present the research we've already paid for once, where is the justice in it all?" Thus, increasingly, funding bodies are demanding that articles based on the research they have paid for must be made available online at no cost a set number of months after being published in a journal.

This open-access journal movement is growing in opposition to the outrageous costs of scholarly journals. Many new journals are being published directly online (after proper peer review) and are available for free to anyone who wants to read them. In this we have the best of the gatekeeping approach of traditional publishing and the free dissemination of information provided by the Internet. For searchable databases of open access journals, go to Open J-Gate (**http://www.openj-gate.com/**) or Directory of Open-Access Journals (**http://www.doaj.org/**).

1.5.3 Government and Corporate Documents

Governments and other corporate groups continue to publish vast amounts of information. Due to the convenience of the WWW as a vehicle for such information, more and more of government information is moving to an online environment where it is usually freely available. For directories to such resources, go to **http://www.lib.umich.edu/govdocs/**.

1.5.4 The World Wide Web

We have already looked at advantages and dangers of the Web. Ongoing issues include use of the Web for highly negative purposes (terrorism, child pornography, etc.), quality challenges which are really evaluation skill problems, the need to catalog the more important Web sites in order to provide more searchability, a demand for search engines that are more able to identify the information we most need, and better instruction for users so that they can optimize the Web experience.

1.5.5 Web 2.0

Web 2.0 is really a concept rather than a defined area of the Internet. If you imagine the average web page to be a publication, a one-way communication from the author to the reader, Web 2.0 forms those parts of the WWW that are interactive. We can include here blogs, wikis, RSS feeds, social networking sites, forums, chat, messaging, e-mail, and so on. As a concept, Web 2.0 doesn't mean too much unless we look at what it does for information.

Take the wiki, cool software that enables you to create web pages that others can edit. One scholarly use for a wiki is in collaborative research projects where several people contribute to an article or some other piece of writing. Another is embodied in Wikipedia, an online encyclopedia that is shaped and revised by its users (and its newer more upscale cousin, Citizendium).

Blogs offer opportunity for one person to post ideas and others to comment on those posts. Forums and chat enable two or more people to share information that can then be revised as the discussion proceeds. Social networking Web sites like MySpace, Facebook and Second Life are enhancing opportunities for people to group-think about information that is of interest to them.

The assumption within Web 2.0 is that connectivity and collaboration create better ideas and make a better world than did one-way communication. This, of course, is not a new insight. Those preliterate people who recounted their history around the campfire so many centuries ago were doing the same thing, but without technology. We need to be careful, however, about not putting Web 2.0 above Web 1.0 and traditional publishing as if collaboration gives our information an edge or credibility that one-way publication could not do. Certainly, a meeting of minds can often result in something better, but that is only the case if the collaborators actually know what they are talking about in the first place.

Truth to tell, much of what you find on Web 2.0 is simply the same old shallow thinking you find in a lot of person to person conversations. Information is no more valuable than the ability of its authors to know something about their subject and to think well. One thing a researcher must guard against is the assumption that because a number of people believe something, it is actually to be believed. Shared opinion is not fact. To move to a level of certainty you can live with, you need to evaluate information by acceptable standards. If you want to see visions of the information world of the future, try these YouTube videos: **http://www.youtube.com/watch?v=xj8ZadKgdC0** and **http://www.youtube.com/watch?v=PY5hBd8_Q-E** (Which I hope will still be there when you read this. If not, search on **Prometeus the media revolution**)

1.6 Primary and Secondary Information Sources

Books and articles that come right from the context of a subject, straight out of the horse's mouth, so to speak, are *primary sources*. Books or articles that comment on a subject area but do not come directly from that subject area are *secondary sources*.

Here are some examples:

Primary	Secondary
Text of Homer's *Iliad*	A modern study of Homer's *Iliad*
A scientific study written by the researcher	Analysis of researcher's experiment
Firsthand account by a witness of 9/11	Book on 9/11 by someone not there
Street person's account of street life	Analysis of research on street people
Text of the Trials of Galileo	Commentary on the Trials of Galileo

Your professor may well want you to consult primary sources on your topic. The key to figuring out what is primary and what is secondary is to ask whether it is an eyewitness account, comes from the subject's time period, is written by a key scholar who developed the subject area, is a direct report of an experiment done by the author of the report, and so on. If so, you have a primary source. If not, you likely have a secondary source. Secondary sources, in general, comment on, analyze or explain the material you would find in a primary source.

1.7 Warning—Not All Information is Informative

We live in a world in which there are many words. The sheer number of words we encounter every day is far greater than it ever has been in all human history. Some of those words come together into information that we can use. Others come together into nonsense. *Not all information is equal.* As you enter the information fog, there are signposts that can help you to discern genuine information from everything else that passes for the real thing. Ask yourself:

➢ What are the qualifications of the author of this information?

➢ Who else believes this?

➢ Has this information been subjected to some kind of peer review or other form of gatekeeping?

➢ Are there vested interests at stake? For example, is that glowing description of the latest mp3 player actually authored by the person who wants to sell it to you and observes that you have money?

➢ What are some good reasons for *not* believing it?

Get ready. We are about to enter the information fog. I hope you enjoy the journey.

1.8 For Further Study

Study Guide

1. How do traditional societies handle information?
2. How did the invention of writing change the pre-writing methods by which a society handled information?
3. Name several significant changes to the world of information brought about by the printing press.
4. In the process of publishing information, what is "gatekeeping" and why is it significant?
5. In what ways is the creation of the World Wide Web a "revolution" for information?
6. In what ways are electronic documents "different" from print ones?
7. Name some advantages of e-books. Why, then, are they still not particularly popular?
8. What is peer review in journal article publishing?
9. What is the open access movement and why was it seen as necessary?
10. Where is the best place to find government documents?
11. What are the advantages and limitations of Web 2.0 for information?
12. Why is not all "information" actually information?

2

Taking Charge

You may be saying to yourself, "I've never been good at this research thing. In fact, I don't think I have a good research project in me."

My response is, "Of course you don't. A good research project is out there, not inside you. What you have to do is get out there, find the data, work with it, and use it to make a difference."

At this point, be aware that we are talking about a certain kind of research here, not the social scientific or scientific research that involves experiments, but informational research such as you will find in the humanities or in literature reviews in the social sciences and sciences. This kind of research is all about data and information, its discovery and use.

Now, before you run off to a dark alley frequented by black market sellers of data, let me offer you a safer alternative. What follows is a list of basic things that you need to have working for you in order to turn your anxiety into a brilliant project, leading to an excellent product.

> ➤ You need an intense desire to do a brilliant project, not just an average one. By definition, most people can do an average project.

> ➤ You need to take your time and plan your research as a *strategy* rather than as a mad dash through libraries and databases. Libraries know when you have reached the panic stage. The books close ranks and refuse to be found. Titles in the catalog trade places so that you can't locate them. The smell of musty books renders you numb and silly. Databases can do even worse things to you (don't ask). *Never panic.* Take it easy. Work out a plan and show that data who's in charge here.

> ➤ You need to become a friend to structure. If you're the kind of person who might follow your schedule if you could remember where you

put it, or someone who views a library overdue fine as a reasonable price to pay for never having to think about a due date, research is going to be a battle for you. Structure and organization, from the beginning of the process all the way to its triumphant end, is crucial, no matter how much pain it will cost you to change your ways.

➤ You need to develop *lateral thinking*. Lateral thinking is akin to what happens in a football game: The quarterback has no openings at all. If he runs with the ball, he'll be flattened. So, instead of moving forward, he throws the ball sideways to another player who can move it forward. These are the steps:

- Recognize that your advance along one line is blocked.

- Abandon your approach and look for another that is completely different.

- Run with your new approach and make it work (or try yet another).

It's like the old story of the truck that got stuck in a highway underpass. No towing vehicle of any kind could get it out, and so the workers were left with the option of dismantling an expensive truck or tearing down an even more expensive underpass until ...

... until the light bulb went on and some bright lateral thinker suggested letting the air out of the truck's tires to *lower* it. Lateral thinking works beyond the obvious, in the realm of the creative.

Nurture this lateral thinking gift within you. It will help greatly in that moment when all your cherished strategies have failed you and you still don't have the information you need.

Here's an example: Suppose you were doing research on the trials of Galileo and discovered that every book with the texts of the verdicts against him was already signed out. Rather than thinking that the library has let you down and you are doomed to wander the streets as a pathetic warning to others, think beyond the library (a lateral) and check to see if someone has posted the verdict transcripts on the Internet (they have: **http://www.law.umkc.edu/faculty/ projects/ftrials/galileo/galileo.html**). That's the sort of thinking that can save you from the disaster which often lurks, ready to bite the unsuspecting.

2.1 Wrestling with a Topic

"I'm writing a history paper on the Lollards. I don't know who they were (and I'm finding it hard to care). When I'm done—if I can find anything in this confusing yet undersized library—I will have a research paper describing the Lollards. It will stress description of the Lollards. Its theme will be 'Describing the Lollards.' The point I will seek to make is that the Lollards can indeed be described."

Exciting, isn't it? Don't those old Lollards just thrill you to pieces? Not really. It's just another research project, as tedious as the last one you did. *Fact is, it isn't even research.*

"What?" you say. "Not research? I searched the library catalog and journal databases and even the Internet, and I've got a ton of stuff here. Don't tell me I'm not doing research."

All right, I won't. Go ahead and write your paper and describe your Lollards. Turn it in and wait for your professor to read the thing and give you the usual dreary mark. Obviously, you don't like your prof anyway, and that's why you keep doing this too him or her. Professors are no strangers to the kinds of boredom you inflict on them. In fact they're almost used to the tedious task of marking your essays. You bore the professor, and the professor pays you back by giving you a C. Any illusion that you actually did research will be dead by the time you get the essay back.

Not wanting to be harsh without providing some help, let me ask: What is genuine research if it's not what you've been passing off? Let's begin by looking at what it is not.

2.2 Elements of False Research

➢ False research assumes that the task is merely to gather data and synthesize it. Thus the typical student "research" project involves amassing data, reading and absorbing it, then regurgitating it back onto a fresh piece of paper (sorry for the disgusting image).

➢ False research deals in generalities and surveys. It loves a superficial look at a big topic, and it abhors depth and analysis.

➢ False research asks no analytical questions and makes no pretense of advancing knowledge. It's happy just to report on what has already been done, to summarize the past.

> ➤ False research is so boring that you should be surprised it ever gets completed, let alone foisted on your longsuffering professor.

2.3 The Key to Genuine Research

What's the point of doing research, then? A flip response might be that a professor or employer told you to do a research project, and you're just following orders. But that's not the answer I'm looking for.

Consider this dilemma as an example: A few years ago you bought a car that was a disaster. Its maker should have been executed for delusions of adequacy. While most cars have water dripping out of the exhaust pipe, yours had lemonade. You spent so much time pushing it that you were able to qualify for a weightlifting competition at the next Olympics. Your mechanic added a new wing onto his house with the money you spent keeping it on the road. Now you're due for a new vehicle, and you are not about to be stung again. So what do you do?

Research!!

You pick up every consumer reporting and car testing book or magazine you can find. You talk to your friends. You go on the Internet. Why? Because you have a burning question to answer, and somewhere out there is the data you need to answer it.

This is what research is all about. The key to genuine research is *a good question.* Without a question, nothing you are doing can be called research. Just as your search through car books is driven by the query, "Which car should I buy this time?" so any research project worthy of its name is driven by a single research question.

What constitutes a good question? Here the situation becomes more complex, because you need to begin rethinking the whole research process. Later in this chapter, we will consider the actual strategies involved in getting a topic ready for research, but for now we need an overview of the basic principles.

The first of these is that most any research topic presented to you needs some work before it is viable enough to use.

Assume, first of all, that the topic is probably too broad to be workable unless you're planning to write a book. A topic like the Lollards or abortion or economic conditions in Russia today is not likely to inspire depth of analysis because you don't have space in ten or twenty pages to deal with anything but the superficial. You are going to have to focus on a more narrow aspect of the topic so that you can deal with it in depth.

Consider a bathtub with a gallon of water in it as opposed to a bathroom sink with a gallon of water in it. Which is deeper? The sink, because its borders are narrower. The same principle works in a research project—the narrower your focus, the more chance you have of getting some depth into your project.

Assume, second, that you are going to have to develop a sound working knowledge of the topic before you're going to know what to do with it. I see a lot of students floundering for hours at the beginning of a project because they really don't understand the basics of the subject matter they are dealing with.

Assume, third, that you may have to negotiate with the one who gave you the project. You need to know that what you propose is actually going to fly with the person ultimately responsible for your fate. But cheer up—professors are generally thrilled by any tiny evidence of creativity in their students. Go to your professor and ask politely, "Would you mind if I pursued *this* issue raised by the Lollards? It looks really interesting." Your professor's heart will turn to mush and he or she will say quietly, "Yes, all right," while inside he or she is shouting, "A new approach! I'm getting a new approach!"

Caution: Don't ever say, "May I write on the Albigenses instead?" This signals the professor that you don't like the Lollards, and you most certainly will end up having to write on the Lollards anyway.

2.4 A Model for Research

What, then, is research all about? Here's a model:

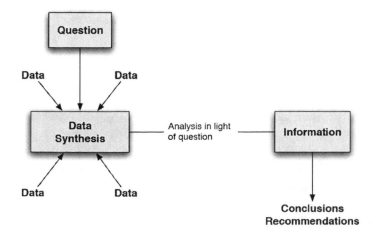

Explanation?

> ➤ You begin with a question.

> ➤ You collect data.

> ➤ You synthesize it (put it together in some coherent form).

> ➤ You analyze it in light of the question (figuring out how each piece of data could be used to answer the question).

> ➤ The analysis turns data into to information (processed data that is ready to be used to answer the question).

> ➤ You come up with conclusions and recommendations.

The key to the whole thing is that *you need to move beyond merely gathering data, reorganizing it (data synthesis) and reporting on what you read.* When a question is injected into the mix, the data becomes more than an end in itself and turns into the raw material needed to answer the question. The result is analysis that turns data into information that can then be used to reach an answer. Looks easy, doesn't it? Maybe it doesn't yet, but we are about to embark on a journey that will make things much clearer.

For a tutorial on the research process, go to **http://www.acts.twu.ca/LBR/ ResearchModel/ResearchModel.swf**

2.5 Getting Started in Research

2.5.1 Getting a Working Knowledge through Reference Sources

Before you go off in all directions at once (like a draw-and-quarter competition at the local jousting match), get a grip on yourself. As I librarian, I see the same painful experience repeated day after day—students walking fearfully into our book stacks area, then stopping, frozen to the ground.

I know what's buzzing through their battered minds: "I'm here, I'm actually here in the library, about to start researching my topic, and I don't have a *clue* what to do. Time has stopped, and people are staring at me. Why can't I move my limbs? Why is my head numb? Maybe I'll die here, rooted to the floor, and they'll bronze me as a monument to the unknown student."

Take heart—it doesn't have to be like this. Let me give you the first step you need to take in any research project, so that you break free from bondage. It's simple. *Get a working knowledge of your topic.*

Right, so what's a working knowledge? Here's a basic definition: *You have a working knowledge of a topic when you can talk about it for one minute without repeating yourself.*

To start your research, all you need to do is acquire one minute's knowledge.

"One minute?" you say. "I've been told I have to present a fifteen page research paper with a dozen footnotes including appropriate journal references (whatever they are). Why talk to me about one minute of working knowledge?" I do so for the same reason that you take a flashlight with you to avoid stumbling around when it's dark. A working knowledge gives you the basics of a topic and enough light so that you won't hurt yourself as you move on into more complicated territory. It isn't complete knowledge, but it's enough to tell you what the topic entails, what its boundaries are, even what some of its controversies, mysteries and dangers might be.

So where do you get a working knowledge? You could simply go on the Internet, where virtually anything is explained by some site or other. But, if you don't know much about the topic to begin with, the Net may be a dubious source. How will you be able to tell that the information is reliable? (We'll cover that issue in Chapter Six).

You would do better to investigate authoritative *reference sources* first. All academic libraries have recognized reference tools that provide concise and authoritative information on virtually any topic you might think of. Reference books will generally appear in the form of dictionaries or encyclopedias on general or specific topics. As well, handbooks, atlases—in fact, any tool that involves looking up brief information—may be found in a reference collection.

Increasingly, reference sources are also appearing in electronic form, allowing for greater flexibility in searching. But you (or your library) will need to subscribe with real money to the best of these. The best reference sources are not available without cost on the Internet, though some older or lite versions of reference tools are appearing there for free. Your most useful venue for good reference information is still a library.

So you're in a library and wondering how to find a reference book that will give you information on marriage customs of the Kurdish people. You could wander the shelves of the reference collection, but there's an easier way to find what you want. *Think of the broad subject within which you topic lies.* In this case, you are looking at customs of a particular culture. Thus you could look up a subject heading in your library's catalog like MANNERS AND CUSTOMS—

ENCYCLOPEDIAS to find a reference source like *Worldmark Encyclopedia of Cultures and Daily Life.* Then just look up "Kurds."

Let's try another example of the sort of material you're looking for in a working knowledge. You've been longing to find out who the Lollards were (or are), admit it. Let me give you a clue—they were a group of religious people who flourished in the late Middle Ages and early Reformation period. What sort of a reference source would you use for Lollards? How about a dictionary of church history? If you check into a couple of such dictionaries, following the famous Five Ws of inquiry, you might discover the following:

Who?

The Lollards were followers of John Wycliffe; more generally, the term was used of any serious critic of the English church in the late Middle Ages. Key figures in the movement were Nicholas of Hereford, William Swinderby, and John Purvey.

What?

Their teachings, summed up by the Twelve Conclusions of 1395, included personal faith, divine election, and the Bible as the sole authority in religion. They demanded that every person have the individual right to read and interpret the Bible.

Where?

The movement existed primarily in England and Scotland.

When?

It began in the 1380s (AD) and went underground after 1431 due to persecution. The movement declined in the mid-1400s but revived about 1490. It figured prominently in the congregational dissent of the seventeenth century and the rise of the Hussites in Bohemia.

Why?

The Lollards claimed to be a reaction to the control over human life and spirituality that was exercised by the Church of the time.

My two reference sources (*Oxford Dictionary of the Christian Church* and *New International Dictionary of the Christian Church*) also yielded a combined bibliography of over 15 sources on the Lollards.

Have I convinced you of the need for a working knowledge? If not, I wish you lots of luck in your research—you're going to need it. Unless you start with a working knowledge you will inevitably find yourself sinking the moment you reach deeper waters.

2.5.2 Excursus: Wikipedia, the Professor's Dilemma

A lot of students have discovered Wikipedia, the free online encyclopedia with an awesome range of articles on every conceivable topic (**http://en.wikipedia.org/wiki/Main_Page**).

Technically speaking, the Wikipedia phenomenon should have been a disaster. Normally encyclopedias are created by an editor who assigns known experts in their fields to write articles that are then carefully studied for accuracy and clarity. Wikipedia's articles are written by the great unwashed—the public, you and me, any Joe or Jane Blow who wants to add an entry. Sure, there are safeguards to help maintain a measure of objectivity and preserve a structure for what is included in a good article. But not only can anyone write an article, anyone can edit an article too. In fact, the edits that actually stick (without being changed back by one of the volunteer watchdogs that guard articles from being vandalized) are those for which a large number of people agree that the change is needed.

Stephen Colbert, the TV satirist, has coined the term "Wikiality." According to Wikipedia: "Colbert defined wikiality as 'truth by consensus' (rather than fact), modeled after the approval-by-consensus format of Wikipedia." (For more fun criticism see the Wikipedia article "Wikipedia in culture.") Colbert, on one of his shows, called on all his viewers to test his "truth by consensus" accusation by changing the entry on Elephants to say that the population of African elephants had tripled in the past six months (it hadn't). Wikipedia had to restrict editing on elephant material due to the large numbers of changes that were made.

All kidding aside, is Wikipedia good or bad? Tough question to answer. The information in it is often amazingly reliable, but there are also glaring errors. Many professors have simply opted for the easiest road and have banned Wikipedia entries from bibliographies. On the other hand, the journal *Nature* did a study that showed the mistakes in Wikipedia to be only a few more than those in *Encyclopedia Britannica*. *Britannica* answered with an angry rebuttal claiming poor methodology, but *Nature* has stuck to is original findings. (*Nature* 438, no. 7070 (December 15, 2005): 900-901; **http://corporate.britannica.com/britannica_nature_response.pdf**).

So, to use or not to use Wikipedia? I am more on the side of "use with discernment as long as your professor allows it (which is often not the case)." If your prof bans it, then you have your answer. If not, recognize that you will likely need to compare the information you find in it with information from sources produced through the usual publishing methods. Keep your wits about you, because you are the gatekeeper.

Above all, check with your professor before you ever include a Wikipedia article in a bibliography.

[For a more in-depth discussion of Wikipedia, see my InfoLitLand column in the March/April 2008 issue of *Online Magazine*].

2.6 Finding a Good Question

Research is not research until you have focused it around a solid research question that addresses a problem or issue. But how do you come up with a question that is going to work?

2.6.1 Narrow your Topic to one aspect. A big reason why research can fail is that the researcher is trying to conquer the world with one project. You simply cannot cover everything about the topic of teen suicide or abortion or the causes of World War One or why the moon *isn't* made of green cheese. You have to choose an aspect that is distinct enough that you can really work with it.

2.6.2 Identify Controversies or Questions related to your narrowed approach. There's no point re-describing what has already been described, since research is not the *gathering* of information but the *use of information to solve a problem*. Information is not an end in itself, but a means to help you solve a problem. To tell me once more who the Lollards were is to do what every reference source on the subject has already done. This is where those excruciatingly boring and superficial "research" papers come from. You must vow never to write another one. Find something worth investigating.

In the case of the Lollards, you might want to focus on one aspect of Lollardy, like the Lollard Knights, and discover why they did not suffer the same persecution as other Lollards (which will lead to the research question). The broader your focus, the more shallow your paper. You want depth. Avoid questions that survey large amounts of data. The resulting papers will never dwell on any one thing for more than a few lines, and they will have bibliographies that cover a wide variety of issues. Instead of looking at all the causes of

WWI, find a crucial cause and analyze it. Narrow is good; big sweeping questions breed ugliness.

2.6.3 Thesis Statements

What if, instead of a research question, you have been asked to provide a *thesis statement?* What's the difference? Research questions and thesis statements are actually two sides of the same coin. A research question addresses a problem to be solved. A thesis statement is *a tentative answer* to a research question. It is tentative in that your written research project is going to have to test your thesis and hopefully show it to be correct. Thus, if you research question were:

To what extent should the government have known of the risk of the New York 9/11 disaster before it happened?

your thesis statement could be:

There was sufficient warning of a New York 9/11-type disaster before it happened, so the government should have been well prepared for its occurrence.

or your thesis might be:

Despite the signs of a potential terrorist attack, there is no way that the government could have had sufficient information to be prepared for the New York 9/11 disaster.

For either of these possible thesis statements the onus would be on you to provide convincing evidence to support your thesis (as well as giving due consideration to contradicting evidence).

The thesis statement route does have a tendency to create a bias, so that it's tempting to overlook or minimize evidence that does not support your case. Thus, unless you have been told to provide a thesis statement, using a research question is likely to have you entering the investigation with a more open mind.

2.6.4 Research Questions—the Bad and the Ugly

Some research questions simply won't work. They are doomed to failure and will produce research projects that are walking disasters, if they can walk at all. One way to recognize a good question is to know what the bad and ugly ones look like, so here are some examples. I am assuming, of course, that these examples will just provide information to use in scorning your classmates, since you, personally, never fall into such traps. [APPENDIX ONE offers you expanded information on the following, along with many more examples]:

1. The Question that Isn't There. Imagine the horror of someone reading your "research" paper and looking desperately but in vain for a question, only to discover that there is none or the question you do have only asks you to compile existing data. What's the purpose of your paper—to tell me something I could have read in any reference book? To tell me once again what everyone knows already? To bore me with your knowledge of trivia?

2. The Fuzzy Question. Sure, there's a question, but it isn't defined or focused enough to make it possible to answer. Asking something like, *Why was Saddam Hussein the way he was?* is no help at all. What way *was* he? Are you talking about his role as dictator of Iraq, his use of chemical weapons, his oil strategy, or just what? Until you clarify your focus, you will find no way to answer your question without simply surveying everything the world knows about him (which would likely depress the life out of you).

3. The Multi-part Question. *You must never let more than one research question intrude into a research project.* The shotgun approach is out. Research identifies *one* question, deals with that question through analytical use of data, and *then quits.* Never *ever* get stuck in the kind of proposal that says, *This paper will deal with_____. I will also attempt to _____ and to_____ and to _____.*
    Your second, third and fourth questions are loose torpedoes on your own ship. They will sink you because they'll kill your focus. One question per research project is all you need or want.

4. The open-ended question. This is often expressed as, *What are the implications of ...* or *What were the results of ...* followed by an expected list of possible outcomes. Open-ended questions tend to be troublesome simply because they fragment your conclusion into many conclusions and thus destroy the single focus you needed to seize upon. The way to cure open-endedness is to *close the end.* For example, instead of asking, *What were the implications of the end of WWII?"* you could ask, *"What crucial factors at the end of WWII led to the recovery of the French automobile industry? Even then the question is somewhat open-ended but at least the focus of the implications is much narrower than it was.*

5. **The Question that Will Not Fly.** Some questions are amazingly inventive, but try to answer questions that the data simply will not answer. Asking: *What is the effect of the growth of the Internet on the prevalence of schizophrenia in the American population?* may look cool, but exactly how would you gather relevant data to answer it? If your question is ambitious, ask yourself whether or not it's possible to find an answer. If not, curb your enthusiasm.

In my experience, the best research questions are *simple* ones that require a good deal of analysis to answer. If you start with a highly complex question, your analysis is going to have to be that much more complex. The ideal is to have a question so simple and clear that you can almost see the goal before you, in your mind's eye, and the path you need to take to get there.

[For more on research questions, including many more examples of both the good and the bad, see APPENDIX ONE.]

2.7 The Preliminary Outline

Chances are, if you're like most people, that you're not in any mood at this point to start thinking about an outline for your project. People who start working on their outline before they've done their first catalog search are either sick or lost souls, because any sensible person knows that you compose your outline AFTER you write your paper.

Wrong.

If you want to spare yourself a ton of grief, start on an outline now. Why? Simply because you need to build yourself as clear a road map as possible in order to do your research efficiently (by "efficiently," I mean that you will save time). A research question may be crucial to give your search a goal, but an outline is crucial to tell you in detail what you need to search for to reach that goal.

What's a preliminary outline? It is simply 3 to 5 points that you need to cover in order to answer the research question. The points may change over time, but you need to start on an outline now.

How do you develop a preliminary outline? Begin with your research question and root your outline in its terminology. Suppose you have the following question: *Why did the US so strongly believe that Saddam Hussein had weapons of mass destruction when the Iraq War of 2003 began?* The question itself gives clues for a preliminary outline. You need to look at possible evidence that he did have such weapons, evidence that he didn't and the reasons why the US found the evidence that he did so compelling.

Once you have a few basic elements, try to organize them into a rough order. For example:

> The Evidence available at the time that Saddam had weapons of mass destruction

> Evidence available at the time that he did not have had such weapons

> Possible explanation why the US believed he had such weapons

> Conclusion

Your preliminary outline is just that—preliminary. You can change it and develop it at will, or even scrap it and create a new one. But you need to start on your outline as soon as you have a research question, because the outline tells you what you need to cover in order to write the paper that answers your research question.

2.8 How About a Few Good Examples?

2.8.1 "The Thought of Erasmus of Rotterdam"

Your much beloved philosophy professor has assigned you "The Thought of Erasmus of Rotterdam." Having studied a few philosophy dictionaries, you narrow your topic to "The Humanism of Erasmus of Rotterdam." You *could*, at this point, decide to begin your paper with "Erasmus of Rotterdam was born in the year …" You *could* go on to explain what he taught about humanism and then conclude, "It is clear that Erasmus was an important person who deserves more attention."

This method is called "regurgitating your sources." It establishes a conduit between your books and your writing hand without ever really engaging your brain. It also makes for a very dull paper. Professors fall asleep over dull papers.

On the other hand, you could be analytical. Having read your sources and affixed your working knowledge firmly in your mind, you could engage your brain in finding a research question. How about asking this: *What is the essential difference between the humanism of Erasmus and that of the modern Humanist Manifestos I and II?* This would certainly demand study of Erasmus, but it would go further. Now your have the makings of an approach that could contribute something fresh and exciting to the topic.

2.8.2 "Homelessness in our Cities"

You are taking a sociology class and are supposed to write a paper on "Homelessness in our Cities." You could regurgitate some statistics, recite a few case studies and conclude, "It is obvious that we need to take action on this issue." Or you might narrow your topic and ask a research question like this one: *Do programs that arrest homeless teens and compel them to accept social worker assistance actually reduce the incidence of teen homelessness in the long run?*

2.8.3 "The Causes of the Ecological Crisis"

For a course on environmental issues, you have been assigned, "The Causes of the Ecological Crisis." You narrow this to focus on the human values in society that can lead to ecological problems. A descriptive paper would string together quotations from current leaders in the debate who are decrying our attitudes of wastefulness and greed. Your conclusion could read, "Thus it is clear that we must change our attitudes." You have narrowed your topic, but you've failed to apply a research question to it. An analytical research paper would go further, perhaps considering the common view that the western Protestant ethic, with its desire for dominion over the earth, is at the heart of the environmental trouble we are in. Your research question could be: *Is Western Protestantism responsible for the environmental crisis?*

2.8.4 "Behaviorism as a Model for Social Engineering"

You have been given a topic which is fairly narrow but still covers a lot of territory. Why not narrow it down to the Behaviorist model of B.F. Skinner? You might now take the easy way and summarize his book *Walden Two*, which is Skinner's model for social engineering (but easy is the way that leads to destruction). Or you could ask how Skinner's model in *Walden Two* might need to be reconsidered if basic human depravity were taken into account (something Skinner seemed blissfully unaware of).

One final note of caution: Always clear your narrowed-down topic and brilliant research question with your professor or supervisor. Disaster could be awaiting you if you don't.

Of course, some of us *like* to flirt with disaster. Do you feel lucky?

2.9 For Further Study

Study Guide

1. What three things do you need to seek if you want to do research well?
2. Name four elements of "false research." Why is each an enemy of true research?
3. Define a "working knowledge" of your topic and explain why it's important to have one.
4. What is a "reference source?"
5. What should we do with Wikipedia?
6. What are the steps to finding a good research question?
7. Formulate a definition for genuine research.
8. Describe the difference between a research question and a thesis statement. Why is the former a safer approach?
9. Describe the following types of bad research questions: The fuzzy question, the multi-part question, the open-ended question, the question that will not fly.

Practice with Research Questions

Go to APPENDIX One and try *A1.2 Practice with Research Questions*

Assignment for a Research Project of Your Own

1. Choose a topic of interest to you.

2. Get basic information about your topic from at least two specialized reference sources (not general encyclopedias but subject specialized reference sources like *Dictionary of Developmental & Educational Psychology*) to provide yourself with a working knowledge of it.

3. Summarize in about half a page what you've learned (your working knowledge), *listing the reference sources you used.* [NOTE: If you could not find a suitable reference source, use an introductory chapter from a recent book. If you can find neither, seek out a reference source on the WWW, but be sure it has authority. **Established reference books either in print or in electronic versions are preferred, however.**]

4. List 4-5 possible research questions related to the topic, in question form, which might be suitable for a research essay. These questions should deal with one aspect of the topic, as narrowly as possible. They should not be easy to answer, nor should they be intended to describe what is already known. Try to make them as analytical as you can.

5. Choose the one question you think is best.

6. Create a preliminary outline.

Teaching Tool

For a short animated tutorial on the research model presented here, go to: http://www.acts.twu.ca/LBR/ResearchModel/ResearchModel.swf

3

Database Searching with Keywords and Hierarchies

It's time to begin traveling into the realm of electronic searching, a land much more complex and (frankly) exciting than you ever imagined when you first Googled something and actually got what you were looking for. So pack your bags. We're going to be out there in the land of search for at least two chapters. On the plus side, by the end of our exploration you're sure to be a better and wiser human being.

3.1 What's a Database?

Chances are that you fancy yourself as a computer genius and the word "database" doesn't sound like "root canal." But this doesn't mean you've learned how to *search* a database quickly and efficiently, coming up with the exact results you need most of the time.

Then again, you may not yet have warmed to computers, nor do you think of them as friendly creatures ever ready to help you, like a big Saint Bernard in avalanche territory. For you, "database" may well be a bad word, a frightening word. If that's your situation, let me give you a soothing message: "Fear not."

Actually, databases are everywhere, and I guarantee you've already searched one or more though not necessarily with all the skill you needed. When was the last time you used a phone book, a dictionary, a library catalog? All of these are databases. Here's a definition:

A database is any collection of data that can be retrieved using organized search procedures.

Phone books are databases of names, addresses and phone numbers. They are set up alphabetically, so that we can use an *organized search procedure* (involving the alphabet) to help us retrieve the data we need. Just to confuse us, however, the Yellow Pages are organized by subject, then by alphabet.

Most common print databases are easy to search. But when databases are in computerized form, a whole new set of problems emerges:

➤ Computer databases are generally much larger than print ones.

➤ There are few common conventions for searching computerized databases, so every new database is a new experience.

➤ Unlike a phone book, you can't really browse a computer database well. It's a black hole into which you are calling: "Please send me the data I want!" Computers, being inherently unintelligent, don't always understand what you want, and frustration sets in quickly. If you use the wrong search technique or poor terminology, the blessed machine may tell you that the data isn't in there when you know full well that it is.

Many people today are hotshots on computers. They can make the keys sing, the mouse roar and the CPU hum. But few of us understand database searching well enough to do it effectively, let alone efficiently.

Case in point—I once found the dregs of a search on a computerized journal database. The database itself had over 1,000,000 article citations listed in it, and this searcher had typed in the keyword *Johnson*, resulting in 4,386 hits. That is, 4,386 descriptive records of journal articles related to the name *Johnson* had become available to him/her. What was worse, the searcher had actually started pulling up each of those 4,386 entries in turn, looking for the right one. Ten hours later, red-eyed, fingers like angry claws ... one can only imagine the *angst* that this session created.

You may know how to use a computer, but disaster will befall you if you don't understand how to search databases. Worry not, however. You're about to discover a few things.

3.2 Keyword Searching

The keyword has become the main tool of research in today's electronic database environment, and many people assume that keywords are their friends.

That's not exactly the case. Have you ever had "friends" you trusted only to a certain point, because you had to tell yourself to watch your back when you were around them? You knew they appeared kind and could be helpful, but they could just as easily betray you or do you harm. That's the keyword—useful, handy, but potentially a backstabber. Keywords represent the Wild West of database searching—bold and exciting, but risky as can be.

In the next chapter we'll look at a more civilized and sophisticated way to search many databases using controlled vocabularies, but for now, let's do what we can to tame the fickle keyword.

3.2.1 Database Basics for Keyword Searching

We start with the principle that every database is made up of words. Computers, though inherently unintelligent when it comes to real thinking, are experts at recognizing words. To understand how keyword searching works, you need to know that most databases use descriptive *records* to identify and show the features of the data they are dealing with. For example, every time a new book is added to a library, it is cataloged by creating a *catalog record,* which might look something like this:

Title: Google and the myth of universal knowledge: a view from Europe
Author: Jeanneney, Jean Noël, 1942– .
Publisher: Chicago: University of Chicago Press, c2007.
Description: xvi, 92 p. ; 23 cm.
ISBN: 9780226395777
Series: Digital formations ; v. 6
Subjects: Google (Firm)
        Library materials—Digitization.
        Electronic information resources—Europe.
        Information organization.
        Digital libraries.
        Web search engines—Europe.
        Internet industry—Europe.
        Internet—Social aspects.

Call No.: ZA4234.G64 J4313 2007

This is, in essence, a description of the main details about this book that the database needs to have available in order for you to identify and find the book. When you search the database by keyword, you will be looking for *significant words* in this record. Now, imagine that there are thousands of records, and you're interested in finding a list of books about the social ramifications of the Internet. You should be able to think of important words (= *keywords*) and input them into a search box. The database search program will then look for those words in each of the *records* in the database and will download to your screen any records that have the words you've asked for.

Suppose that we wanted to find materials on interactive aspects of Internet use. In this case, your search might look like this:

Interact* and Internet (Don't worry about the search form yet. We'll get to the details below).

You will get records for books with titles like:

- *Social consequences of Internet use: access, involvement and interaction*
- *Digital borderlands: cultural studies of identity and interactivity on the Internet*
- *Murder on the Net: a guide to logging on and using the Internet via an interactive murder mystery adventure*

(All of the above are real titles of real books)

Rule #1: *With keyword searching, what you type is what you get. The computer cannot interpret your request or give you the next best solution (though some may search on a few synonyms). All it can do is identify the words you ask for and give you the relevant data. Garbage in, garbage out.*

Notice one little trick I performed above—*truncation* (sometimes inaccurately called *wildcards*). With many keyword searches, you can type part of a word, then add an asterisk (*) or sometimes a question mark (?), and the computer will look for every word that begins with the letters you typed. E.g., **interact*** will ask the computer to search for **interact, interacting, interaction,** even **interactivity.**

You can also sometimes do *forward truncation* in which the asterisk goes at the beginning (rare) or *middle truncation* (the real meaning of "wildcards"), in which truncation is done within a word (e.g., Wom*n).

Even given the variations allowed through truncation, keyword searching demands a whole lot of precision. The search function in the computer database will only find the exact thing you want it to find. If you mistakenly type **intract*** instead of **interact***, the search function will give you data with the word **intractable**, thus spoiling your whole day and making you grouchy in social environments. So do what your mother told you and learn to spell. Get it right the first time.

3.2.2 Boolean Searching

Many years before computers, a man named George Boole invented a mathematical system that enabled people to visualize the combination of various classes of things. The computer folks have taken his system into the world of database searching in order to formulate searches where two or more terms are used. Let's look at some of the basic commands used in Boolean searching:

The OR Command

Suppose that I'm looking in a database for information about cars. I realize that a keyword search will pull out all information that has the word "cars" in it, but some people use the term "automobiles." How can I tell the database search program to look for *both* words at the same time and give me data whether that data uses the word "cars" *or* the word "automobiles?"

In a situation in which I am searching for synonyms—different words that mean the same thing—I use the OR command. Let's visualize it this way:

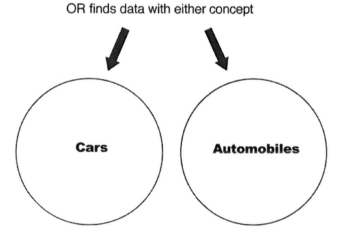

OR finds data with either concept

Cars   Automobiles

That is, "Database Search Program, please give me everything on cars or automobiles, I don't care which." So you will get all the data with "cars" in it, plus all the data with "automobiles" in it. Both words don't have to be in your results. Either word will do.

In a keyword search in a computer catalog or some other database, your search may look like this:

Cars or Automobiles

Another situation calling for an **OR** search might be that in which two concepts are closely related, and you suspect that finding data on either of them will further your overall goal. For example, in doing a search for "psychoanalysis" you might also want to search for the father of psychoanalysis—Sigmund Freud. If you leave off the "Sigmund" (because he is usually referred to just as "Freud"), you can formulate a search like this:

Psychoanalysis or Freud

With an **OR** search, you typically get a lot of "hits", that is, pieces of data brought down to you out of the database.

Rule #2: *An OR search is usually for synonyms or for keywords that are already closely related. You use it to anticipate the various ways something might be described or approached so that you don't have to do multiple individual word searches.*

The only alternative to doing an OR search is to do separate searches on each of your search terms, then try to compile the various sets of results. OR lets you avoid the pain of such an experience.

The AND Command

One of the most profitable uses of keywords is in combining topics to narrow down a search. For example, if you wanted to look at the problem of educating homeless youth, a keyword search could be formulated to produce very precise results.

Let's visualize it with a diagram first. If you're searching for the relationship between homeless youth and education, you don't want every piece of data on homeless youth, nor do you want every piece of data about education. You want the data that comes from having homeless youth and education intersect. Thus:

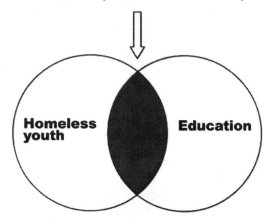

AND finds only data with both concepts

Your formulated keyword search will look like this:

homeless youth and education

A little tip: Be very careful not to add unnecessary words to AND searches. Suppose that you were searching for material in a database on Osama bin Laden's influence surrounding the Iraq War of 2003, (including his supposed alliance with Saddam Hussein). The temptation might be to load up your search with terminology, along the lines of:

Osama bin Laden and Iraq War and 2003 and influence

But stop and think (a nasty exercise, yet required occasionally)—you are searching for *keywords*, probably in a title. Are all these words likely to appear in a title, along the lines of "The Influence of Osama bin Laden Surrounding the Iraq War of 2003?" What if the database had an article whose title went along the lines of "Bin Laden and the Iraq War?" It's on target as far as your search goals are concerned, but your multiword search above is going to eliminate this article from the result list. Why? Because the article doesn't have the words **Osama** and **influence**, nor the date **2003**, in its title. In other words, you eliminated a good article by demanding that too much terminology appear in each result you got.

How do you solve a problem like this? By becoming a minimalist:

Rule #3: *In an AND search, always look for the fewest number of terms required to get data that is on target with your search goals. The more unnecessary terms you add, the more you risk screening out good data that does not use those terms.*

For the search above, all you really need is:

Bin Laden and Iraq War

You might even be able to get rid of **Bin.** The "2003" isn't needed either, because Bin Laden had little involvement in the 1990 Iraq war (other than wanting the Saudis to handle Saddam themselves instead of having the Americans do it).

Rule #4: *A keyword AND search is used to search for data that relates two or more topics or concepts together. The data found will show the effect of the relationship between/among these topics.*

An **AND** search is a limiting kind of search. It asks the search program to provide data only when that data contains *all* the keywords linked by **AND.** Thus, you should expect that an **AND** search will give you fewer hits than if you had searched each keyword on its own. This can be a difficult concept to grasp. If you're having trouble with it, go back up to the **AND** search diagram above. Or consider the example above: you don't want every piece of data about Bin Laden plus every piece of data about the Iraq War. You want only the data that *relates* Bin Laden to the Iraq War. Thus the **AND** search has set limits for your search. It has narrowed down the data that you want to receive.

Rule #5: *AND searches will narrow or limit your topic. Thus you can expect that you will not get as many "hits" with an AND search as with an OR search.*

Nesting ANDs and ORs

There are times when, within your AND search, several synonyms of key terms are possible. Unless you enjoy doing multiple searches, you can combine synonyms into one search by "nesting" ORs within an AND search:

Homeless and (youth or adolescen*) and (education or school*)

This might look like it's contradicting the caution I just gave about avoiding over-complicated searches, but there are actually only three word sets that are linked with AND. The rest is alternate terminology using OR, which will not eliminate relevant articles.

Notice that I put parentheses around (i.e., "nested") the OR terms that belong together, because search programs can get confused easily. The parentheses make it clear to the computer how to conduct the search. Notice as well that I truncated adolescen* to hit "adolescent" and "adolescence" and "adolescents." I also truncated "school" to cover "schools" and "schooling."

The NOT Command

If I'm back to looking for information about cars, but I'm *not* interested in any car made in Europe, a NOT search is what I need (Please don't send me cards and letters asking why I have a problem with European cars—it's a long story). With this search, I want to tell the computer to give me everything about cars but no data about European cars. Here's how to do a NOT search:

(cars or automobiles) not Europe*

Notice what I've done. First, I remembered that "automobiles" is a synonym for "cars." Thus I included both, nesting them with parentheses so as not to confuse the computer as to what I meant by my **NOT** command. Then I added the **NOT** and did a truncation on Europe (using an asterisk) so the computer could look for "Europe" and "European" with a single search. What I'm saying is that I want data about either cars or automobiles as long I don't have to deal with European cars or automobiles.

Exceptions to the Above

Exceptions? Why are there always exceptions? Probably because every database likes to do its own thing. Here are some variations of the standard Boolean **OR, AND, NOT** searches:

> ➢ In many databases, you can do an **AND** search simply by leaving a space between words. Instead of:
>
> **homeless youth and education**
>
> you can type:
>
> **homeless youth education**

➤ But note that some other databases will see homeless youth education as a single phrase, thus requiring you to put the AND back in between "youth" and "education.

➤ A *very* small number of the less sophisticated Internet search Engines use + instead of the normal automatic "and". Thus

+"homeless youth" +education *[= homeless youth and education]*

➤ In some databases, **NOT** has to be expressed as **AND NOT**. In Internet search engines, not is generally expressed with a hyphen before a word, with no spaces:

-European

➤ Many databases ask you to put quotation marks around words that need to appear together, e.g.:

"apple trees"

Others call for parentheses: (apple trees).

➤ There are some databases now that actually search for synonyms of the term(s) you input so that they can bring up material you might not have found through a simple keyword search.

➤ Some databases provide a choice of buttons under the search box, like the first example below (representing OR, AND and phrase searches). Others will use a search grid with drop-down boxes like the second example:

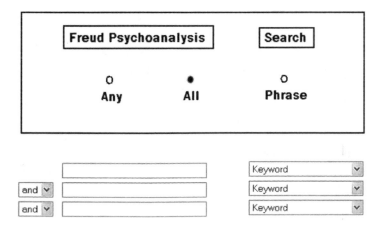

3.3 Keyword Searching with Hierarchies

Keywords are flat. What do I mean? Keyword search engines scan across the broad surface of databases looking for matches. I type in "Iraq" and the search engine finds the word "Iraq." In some results, Iraq is the main topic. In others it is incidental to whatever the data is actually about. Sometimes the results are about the culture of Iraq, sometimes the people of Iraq, sometimes the sad recent history of Iraq. Because keywords are flat—simply appearing where they appear without revealing possible depths of context and meaning—keyword search engines bring up all occurrences of a word, regardless of what surrounding meaning or definition is present. This can be a problem, because knowledge is not flat but hierarchical.

3.3.1 Hierarchies

I know this is starting to look technical, but it's not really. Let's start with a brief look at how knowledge is organized. Put quite simply (because I'm not capable of much beyond simplicity), every bit of knowledge has a context within which it fits. The way the whole of knowledge is organized is from broad categories (at the top) to narrow categories (at the bottom). The broad categories help to define the meaning and boundaries of the narrow ones. Let me illustrate:

Here's a question: Can you define the following word?

ROCK

"Sure," you say. "It's a hard object that comes out of the ground."
To which I answer, "How wrong you are! Don't you know that 'rock' is a verb?" My definition, a symptom of my growing age, is that the only rock worth anything is the rock I do in my rocking chair.
"I'm not wrong," you retort. "You're wrong."
To which your friend standing next to us says with a smirk, "You're both wrong. It's music. Classic Rock is real music, and I'd rather be listening to it than wasting time listening to you argue about word meanings."
What's the problem here? Why can't we agree on a definition for one word with only four letters in it? The reason is simple: If I say, "I'm planning to take a whole evening to rock in my rocking chair," you know that my definition of 'rock' is something like 'a back and forth motion.' If, on the other hand, I say,

"The rock that went through my window was two inches across," you know that 'rock' is now a noun meaning 'a hard substance taken from the earth.'

Words by themselves don't really mean anything for certain. They only have a definite meaning when you put them in a context. Words get their meaning from the sentences surrounding them. In turn, sentences become understandable within their paragraphs, and paragraphs make sense within the larger context of the complete document. The important word here is "context." Meaning is derived from context, and without context we have only confusion.

So what? How do meaning and context relate to research? Exactly like this: All data exists within one or more information hierarchies (contexts). Let me illustrate with the word "rock."

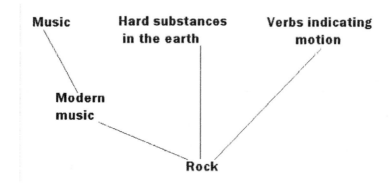

"Rock" is a sub-class of more comprehensive categories. For example, "rock" may be a sub-class of modern music, right alongside other sub-classes like "adult contemporary," "elevator music," and the compositions of John Cage. "Modern music" in turn is a sub-class of the larger category of "music" along with other sub-classes like "classical," "baroque," etc. What we end up with is a hierarchy. Each higher grouping is broader than the one below it.

But notice that "rock" is capable of having several different hierarchies attached to it, depending on the meaning we give to the word. It can also be a sub-class of "hard substances in the earth" or of "verbs indicating motion."

All data comes within a context. Without context the data cannot tell us what we need to know. Few concepts, however, are bound within a single context but are capable of belonging to a number of possible contexts.

Let's now move into an area that better resembles a research topic. Take something like the Roman emperor Constantine. Depending on how you approach him, he can exist within a number of contexts (= hierarchies):

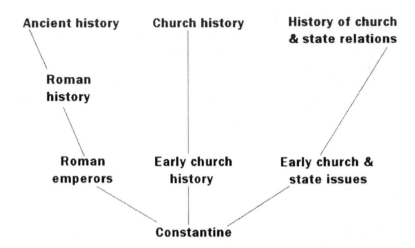

You can deal with him as a sub-class of "Roman emperors" alongside other sub-classes like Julius Caesar and Nero. "Roman emperors" in turn are a sub-class of "Roman history", which in turn is a sub-class of "Ancient History." Alternatively, you can deal with him as an important figure within the larger subject of "Early Christian Church History," since he was the emperor who affirmed Christianity so that it could eventually become the official Roman religion. Or you can discuss him within the higher class of "History of Church and State," since his marriage between empire and the Church led to many issues related to the wisdom of creating such unions. Each of these hierarchies leads to a different approach to the same topic.

All information is hierarchical. The rule is simply this:

Rule #6: *In research, data is only meaningful when you understand the hierarchy (context) within which it is found. You must always know where your data fits within the hierarchy.*

What higher class (context) does your topic belong to in the particular situation in which you find yourself? Are there other hierarchies your topic could belong to? Are there sub-classes of your topic that could become factors to consider?

3.3.2 Clustering Search Tools

Most traditional search engines on the World Wide Web (including Google and Yahoo) do a flat search for keywords thus separating results from their possible hierarchies. For example, if I search for "William Badke" in Google, I get a bunch of Web site links to all aspects of me (frightening, isn't it?). But those results don't distinguish between Badke the writer, Badke the librarian, Badke the faculty member, Badke the blogger, and so on. Badke is always only Badke (sigh).

A few tools are attempting to do something about this. Let's look at each one in turn:

Clusty (http://clusty.com/)

Through the magic of corporate decision-making, the Internet search engine Vivisimo is now named after its internal working program—Clusty.

When I do a search on "William Badke," it first asks me if I really mean "William Badge" (my humbling experience for the day), then it lists in a side column the following:

> Research Strategies (39)
> Hitchhiker's Guide to the Meaning of Everything (22)
> Trinity Western University (26)
> Ben Sylvester Mystery (13)
> Course (8)
> Style, Writing Research Essays (9)
> Education (5)
> New Books, Back-In-Print Books (3)
> Research Resources

This tool (actually a metasearch engine) has pulled key subject language out of my flat search, subject language that can group my results by the context (hierarchy) within which it exists. Thus Web sites related to my book *Research Strategies* (39 of them) are grouped together in that context. Web sites about my book *The Hitchhiker's Guide to the Meaning of Everything* are grouped together as well. Then comes my connection with Trinity Western University, and so on. Some results are in the upper part of the hierarchy and some in the lower part, so that if we put it into a chart it would look like this:

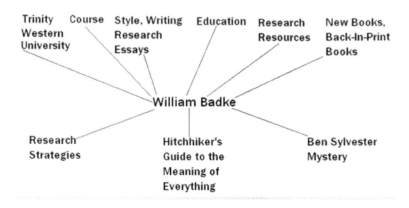

Trinity   Course   Style, Writing   Education   Research   New Books,
Western   Research   Resources   Back-In-Print
University   Essays   Books

William Badke

Research   Hitchhiker's   Ben Sylvester
Strategies   Guide to the   Mystery
                      Meaning of
                      Everything

Thus I am a part of some larger things (like a university), but some things are a part of me (like my mystery series). The clustering puts the flat keyword search into several contexts in the Hierarchy of Me, thus helping you, the searcher, to define more clearly what exactly about William Badke we are looking for.

Quintura (http://www.quintura.com/)

Quintura (launched in early 2007) is similar to Clusty in concept but has a very neat mouse-over feature. Having done an initial keyword search, you can run your mouse over the clustering words on the left to allow the clustering to re-form, giving you even narrower results. What is more, the websites related to whatever word you're mousing over show up in a list on the right automatically. Quintura's gutsy slogan is, "We are not afraid of Google!" (My thanks to my former student Glenn Davies for discovering this interesting tool for me.)

Grokker (http://www.grokker.com/)

Grokker at first looks a lot like Clusty in the way it clusters results, but Grokker has a difference. For several years it operated as a commercial search engine for corporations that paid to have Grokker technology incorporated (pun intended) into their search programs. Now it's available free.

So what does Grokker have that Clusty lacks? It has a visual search tool. First you input a keyword or two. For example, you might type in the word **Globalization**. The result will be a large circle on the screen, representing globalization in total. Within the large circle will be several smaller circles representing aspects of globalization, like foreign policy or economics. Click on any one of these circles and you will be connected to Web sites that deal with the particular aspect of globalization you are interested in.

Grokker is more complex than I've revealed (as is everything, it seems), allowing for special filtering, configuration, and so on. So experiment with it. Such hierarchical tools are still not perfect, because they depend on software to distinguish contexts out of the results you get from your initial keyword search. We all know that computer software lacks the sophistication found in a human brain. Still, clustering tools like this one may well be the future of keyword searching.

The process to use Grokker's Internet search engine site is to input your keyword, "grok" it, and click on "Map View." You may be asked to download some plugins, but they are safe, so fear not.

EBSCO Databases (Your Library or http://www.epnet.com)

One further example of hierarchical searching comes from the EBSCO databases. After a keyword search, your results come accompanied with contexts suggested on the side. Each of these will narrow the search by putting your initial keyword into a particular hierarchy:

Clicking on INTERNATIONAL trade, for example, will create an AND search for globalization and the subject heading "International trade."

EBSCO in early 2008 came out with a new visual search in two possible formats that reflects a lot of the features of hierarchical searching.

3.4 Keyword Searching—The Good, Bad, and Ugly

The good part of keyword searching is that it is quick and flexible as well as giving you the opportunity to narrow down to specific topic areas or combine concepts from more than one subject discipline.

The bad is that you are controlled by the tyranny of words. What do I mean? Simply that different words often can mean much the same thing or a single word (e.g., rock) can be capable of a lot of possible meanings. Keywords as search tools are slippery and can easily betray you.

The ugly is that keywords are flat. They aren't capable of telling you whether your result is broad or narrow in relation to your topic, nor can they spell out the contexts within which your keyword might be found. Clustering search engines try to overcome this problem by suggesting contexts that form hierarchies within which your keyword can live.

So use keywords but be aware that they are not superheroes. In fact, that designation may well go to controlled vocabularies, our next topic.

3.5 For Further Study

Study Guide

1. What is a "database?" Name a few examples of familiar databases.
2. You can browse a paper form telephone book easily. Why is a computer database more difficult to browse than a paper format database?
3. In keyword searching, what strong ability of computers is used?
4. What is a "truncation" or "wildcard?" Give an example along with the appropriate symbol.
5. Explain the "OR command" in Boolean searching and indicate in what types of searches it works best.

6. Explain the "AND command" in Boolean searching and indicate in what types of searches it works best.
7. Explain the "NOT command" in Boolean searching and indicate in what types of searches it works best.
8. Some databases will allow you to leave out the Boolean AND, and just input keywords with spaces between them. In other databases, if you do this the computer program will understand that you are constructing a _____.
9. Why do words by themselves have no definite meaning? How do they get a meaning?
10. All data comes within a _____.
11. Explain an "information hierarchy." Choose two or three topics and illustrate how each fits into one or more hierarchies (a diagram works best for this).
12. In research you must know where you are ____ _____ _____.
13. What does it mean to say that keywords are "flat?"
14. How do clustering search tools like Clusty and Grokker help to resolve the problem of the flatness of keywords?

Practice with Keywords and Hierarchies

1. How would you formulate a keyword search to get results in a database on the following?

   a. The causes of World War One.
   b. Destruction of the museums in Iraq during the 2003 war.
   c. The role of crime in the novel, *The Great Gatsby*
   d. The problem of fear in patients with the psychological disorder paranoia.
   e. Teen violence.
   f. The movie, *Vanilla Sky* (as opposed to the painting, *Vanilla Sky*).
   g. Kidney stones in Schnauzers.
   h. Racial conflict in London.
   i. Relationship between unemployment and homelessness in San Diego.
   j. Stravinsky's musical composition, *The Rite of Spring*.

2. Try searches on Clusty (**http://clusty.com/**), Quintura (**http://www.quintura.com/**) and Grokker's "Map View" (**http://www.grokker.com/**), starting with the keywords **Napoleon Dynamite** in order to discover a review for the movie *Napoleon Dynamite*.

3. Create some hierarchical diagrams for the following: *Microsoft, Iraq, Arnold Schwarzenegger, and Anorexia.* Indicate three possible higher contexts and three lower.

Suggested Key to Practice with Keywords

1. Keyword Search Terms (My Suggestions)

    a. *The causes of World War One*: This is actually a tough one because you can call this war **World War One, World War I, WWI,** and even **The Great War.** Most of these descriptors are actually phrases, and it may be hard to combine them in a search in a database while maintaining their identity as phrases. You may have to search each possibility in turn, e.g., **World War One AND Cause*** (notice the truncation), **World War I AND Cause***, and so on.

    b. *Destruction of the museums in Iraq during the 2003 war*: Likely you can get by here with as little as **Museum* AND Iraq AND War.** Don't worry about the 2003, since the 1990 Iraq war did not raise the issue of museums, so the database will have no problem distinguishing the two wars.

    c. *The role of crime in the novel,* The Great Gatsby: The name Gatsby is rare. In this case, you don't need to fill the search with terms. Simply try **Gatsby AND Crime.**

    d. *The problem of fear in patients with the psychological disorder paranoia*: You have a challenge with the term Paranoia, since it is widely used in contexts other than psychology. Thus, a search like **Paranoia AND Fear** could create a lot of irrelevant hits, among which will be a few that deal with the psychological disorder variety of paranoia. But don't think adding terminology like **Psychological Disorder** will help the situation. It won't, simply because keyword searches look for *words*. It's unlikely that the writers of an article on fear issues in the psychological disorder of paranoia will use the title, "Fear Issues in the Psychological Disorder of Paranoia." The title will much more likely be "Fear in Paranoia," or something similar. Our discussion of controlled vocabularies in the next chapter may add some light to the issue.

e. *Teen violence*: Try (**Teen* OR Adolescen* OR Youth) AND violence.** Note the use of truncation and the choice of synonyms in a nested OR search.

f. *The movie,* Vanilla Sky *(as opposed to the painting,* Vanilla Sky*)*: Try **Vanilla Sky AND Movie**, or even **Vanilla Sky AND Cruise** [because the movie starred Tom Cruise.]

g. *Kidney stones in Schnauzers*: You could try **Kidney AND Schnauzers**. If that generates too many useless results, try **Kidney Stones AND Schnauzers**. With AND searches, always try to make it as simple a process as possible.

h. *Racial conflict in London:* Try **Race AND London**, but there is a potential that "race" may bring up material on racing. Perhaps **Racial AND London** would work more effectively. Avoid adding terminology like Problems, Issues, and so on, since title terminology of your data rarely uses such terms.

i. *Relationship between unemployment and homelessness in San Diego*: Try **Unemploy* AND Homeless* AND San Diego**. [Note that if you are trying this in an Internet search engine, most don't use truncation (*), so you will need to spell out the whole word.]

j. *Stravinsky's musical composition,* The Rite of Spring: For this one, continue the principle that short and simple is better than filling a search with terminology. Since this composition is distinctive, **Rite of Spring** should be enough. If it's not, add **AND Stravinsky**.

2. In this case, you will start with a search on **Napoleon Dynamite** in Clusty or Quintura, then look for the link on the side that will lead you to reviews. With Grokker, you start with the keyword **Napoleon Dynamite**, specify Map View, and look for the circle that says "Film."

3. *Microsoft*—higher categories: Computer software, competition laws, successful companies. Lower categories: Office 2003, recent court cases seeking to break up Microsoft, secrets of Microsoft's success as a company.

Iraq—higher categories: Archaeology, Arab Nations, history of war. Lower categories: Destruction of museums in Iraq in 2003, Iraq's relations with Iran, the Iraq war of 2003.

Arnold Schwarzenegger—higher categories: Body building, movie actors, politicians. Lower categories: Arnold's methods to stay in shape, Arnold as comic actor, the 2003 California recall election.

Anorexia—higher categories: Weight loss, psychological conditions, social problems. Lower categories: The effects of weight loss in those with anorexia, the role of a certain life factor in anorexia, the role of "thin culture" in the increase in anorexia.

Assignment for a Research Project of Your Own

1. State a research question on a topic of your choice. Have a good look at it and determine exactly what you want to search for

2. Do a *title keyword* search for books in a library catalog by:
    a. Choosing important words related to your topic, and doing searches by these words either individually or in Boolean combinations. *Indicate the actual searches you tried, e.g.,* (**Skinner or behaviorism**) **and Walden.**
    b. Listing 8-10 books, *relevant* to your topic, which you identified through your keyword search. Keep as narrowly focused on your research question goal as possible.

4

Metadata and the Power of Controlled Vocabularies

The terminology of this chapter title may have you quivering, but you're about to learn some cool words to impress your friends and some cooler concepts to make you a better searcher than you ever could have been with keywords alone.

I do have to lay a bit of theory on you, though. Sorry about that. Theory seems too often like joining a fraternity. You know it'll look great on your resume, but the initiation might be more frightening than the potential membership benefits. In this case, however, understanding a few basics will help the rest of the chapter make sense.

4.1 It's All about the Metadata

Research is a quest that often has you trekking into strange territory so that you can harvest the information you need and resolve the problem posed by your research question. This is the task of "search," and these days, as you know, search is done with a computer.

If you are devoted Googler (or Yahooer, or whatever) you already know about the joys and sorrows of search. One disturbing fact emerges, though— search is a messy thing, often leaving you with far more that you *don't* need than the little you do. So you find yourself saying to the computer, "No, no, no, I want *this*, not *that*, you blockhead machine."

And it is exactly that—a blockhead, I mean. Computers are not intelligent creatures. They recognize letters and words, and they can find exactly what you type into the search box. They don't know whether or not the actual information is irrelevant even though it contains your search words. In fact, they don't even know what your words mean.

Now imagine that you're doing a research project looking for Web sites dealing with Google's plans for YouTube. So you go to the Google search engine and type in **Google YouTube plans.** You do get a number of news sources on Google's plans for YouTube, but you're not really interested in news. You'd prefer a statement directly from Google about its plans.

So now you search **Google YouTube plans "directly from Google"** (using quotation marks to search it as a phrase). Disaster. Nothing in the list is what you're seeking. What went wrong? Metadata trouble, that's what.

In this chapter I want to take you into the guts of the machine to understand why some searches succeed and others fail. I want you to get a grasp why some databases work better than others and why it has everything to do with the way those databases are constructed. So here goes …

4.2 Understanding Metadata

I want to avoid throwing complicated terminology at you, because you get enough of that in the normal course of your life, but "metadata" is a cool concept, and knowing what it means can make you a winner at a party when you're trying to convince other people that you are a "somebody." To understand metadata, you need to understand how databases are constructed.

Any database is only as useful as its retrieval capability. If you can't get out what you need when you need it, then what you have is a data warehouse, not a database. For some databases, and for much of the WWW, retrieval is done solely through keywords in the data itself. This, as we will see, is a pretty inefficient way to find specific pieces of information.

Enter metadata. If a database constructor wants to be successful in setting up data for retrieval, good metadata will do the trick. Consider this fictional listing from a phone book:

Smith, Harley Q. 2947 Olivier Ave., Anytown, WA. 699-555-4023

This is a name, address and phone number for one listing in a phone book. Now, suppose that I have digitized the phone book and I've made the text of it searchable online. A user wants Harley Smith's phone number. To do so he/she could construct the following keyword search:

Harley Smith

Here are the results:

Boyton, **Harley**, 7690 **Smith** St., Clumpers, MN. 908-555-2956
Harley, John, 2187 Jones St., **Smith**, ND 867-555-4289
Smith, Amos, 2798 **Harley** Rd., Johnstown, AR 223-555-1972
Smith, Douglas, 1197 Samuels Ave., **Harley**, CN. 256-555-6843
Smith, **Harley** Q. 2947 Olivier Ave., Anytown, WA. 699-555-4023

You can see that this database isn't very concerned about word order or word proximity, and that it doesn't know a personal name from a street name. It doesn't know if Harley is the first name of a person or the name of a town. The keywords are all there, but you got five results instead of one and most of them are not what you were looking for.

So what was the problem? A lack of metadata. The database search engine is simply looking for your search words in a sea of undifferentiated text.

Now let's show you how a smart phone number database would set up an entry (as most do):

Name: Smith, Harley Q.
Street: 2947 Olivier Ave.
City: Anytown
State: WA
Phone: 699-555-4023

Every part (or "field") of the above entry is encoded with identifiers (e.g., Name, Street, City) that distinguish between the various parts of this data record. The encoding is metadata—that is, a system of codes or identifiers that comes along with the data. Now, when you enter a search in an online version of this phone listing, your search box might look like this:

Enter the following information:

Name	Smith, Harley
Street	
City	
State	WA

This would get you:

Smith, Harley Q. 2947 Olivier Ave., Anytown, WA. 699-555-4023

Only one Harley Smith. No longer are you buried in the kind of confusion we saw in the first example above. Why not? Because the database creators inserted *metadata* to distinguish names from street addresses from cities. Now the database knows the difference between a personal name and a city or street name, so you get results much closer to what you are actually looking for.

4.3 Excursus: An Analogy that Might Help (or not)

I've set this one as an excursus (a neat digression) because I'm not entirely sure it will help. Skip it if you want, but I think you'll benefit from hanging in here.

Think of a supermarket—row after row of products. Each row has end-signs indicating what types of things they contain—baby food, breakfast cereal, and so on. Each of the products on the shelves, as well, is labeled in some way.

Now, imagine that I take away the signs at the ends of each row. To compound my nasty work, I replace the names and brands on all products with simple lists of ingredients.

Suppose, then, that you go looking a particular brand of chicken soup that used to have a label that said "Chicken Soup" and had the brand icon for *Mrs. Murphy's Delicious Foods.* Because I have removed the signposts and labels, all you find now is undefined shelf after shelf of products with white labels that read, "Chicken pieces, carrots, beans, MSG, broth, salt," and so on. There are no shelf markers telling you where the soups are. There are no labels identifying the type of product (Chicken Soup) nor are there any brand designations.

If that were your shopping experience, you'd be rattled. All the important signposts and indicators would be gone, leaving you to search, without the help of identifiers, through a vast number of products, hoping to find the specific things you need.

Here's the analogy: The signs at the ends of the rows are like subject indicators in metadata records within a database—they tell you what type of data you are dealing with (cereals, vegetables, etc.) The product names are like titles that identify particular pieces of data. The brand names are like author identifications on pieces of data, showing who produced them.

Without signs and identifier labels, all you have is lists of ingredients that may or may not help you find the chicken soup you are longing for. Metadata is comprised of all the labels that enable you to find the right row and the right product in that row simply and easily.

4.4 Metadata in Practice

Let's see how metadata works in the research process. For most databases, but not the searchable part of the WWW, the database search engine doesn't really look for the data itself but searches metadata. The metadata comes in the form of a "record," that is, *a short description of the data.* If the data were books in a library, the metadata would be the "records" that describe each book, and that would be what the catalog's search engine would look for. The same would be true of a computerized database that searches for journal articles, though these days, because so many journal articles are in electronic form, it is possible to search the full text of articles as well as the metadata records.

Back in 2003 I published a book entitled *Beyond the Answer Sheet: Academic Success for International Students* (great book by the way; you owe it to yourself to get a copy and make me rich). Shortly after publication, a library catalog record (metadata) was produced for the book. It looked like this:

LDR: 00793nam 2200265Ia 45x0
005: 20030610113341.0
008: 030610s2003 nyua 001 0 eng d
020: $a 0595271960
035: $a ocm52399619
090: $a LB2375 $b .B33 2003
100: 1 $a Badke, William B., $d 1949–
245: 10 $a Beyond the answer sheet: $b academic success for international students/$c William B. Badke.
260: $a New York: $b iUniverse, $c c2003.
300: $a v, 152 p. : $b ill. ; $c 24 cm.
500: $a Includes index.
650: 0 $a Academic achievement.
650: 0 $a Foreign study.
650: 0 $a College student orientation.
650: 0 $a Student adjustment.
650: 0 $a College students.
650: 0 $a Students, Foreign $x Education (Higher)

A lot of this record looks like meaningless code, but some of it is fairly easy to understand. The number 100, for example, designates the author of the book, and 245 the title. Thus, if we had a library catalog search engine that could be set to search only within 100 fields for authors, it should be able to pick up a list of all the books I've written that are located in the particular library I am searching. The search engine doesn't search through the whole record but goes directly to the 100 (author) field and searches only that field in every record in the database, looking for my name. Thus the database truly knows the difference between an author and a title, because the metadata is set up to distinguish these things.

Metadata records range from the good to the bad to the ugly to the nonexistent. In general, the more effort database producers take to develop metadata, the better chance the user will have of finding what he/she actually wants to find. If you do a Google or Yahoo search, it becomes obvious right away that there is no search box to look for authors of Web sites or titles of Web sites or even for types of Web sites (e.g., reviews of Toyota cars as opposed to Toyota's corporate Web site). This isn't the search engine's fault. Most Web sites just don't have the encoded metadata to enable such a search to be done.

Lack of metadata leads to tons of search results, but you have to do a large amount sifting to find a match with what you were searching for. If you search a library catalog, on the other hand, you will find that there is an available author search, a title search, a subject heading search, etc. that can help you nail down what you are looking for. Why? Because the library catalog is made up of metadata records.

Even with adequate metadata, the big problem with computer databases is not with getting information into them, but with *retrieving* the information you need. For this purpose, there are two basic search tools available to you: *keywords* and *controlled vocabularies*. We looked at the former in the previous chapter, so now we need to turn to the latter, which depends totally on metadata.

4.5 Controlled Vocabularies

A few years ago, as people started sharing things on the WWW (photos, favorite bookmarks, etc.), *folksonomies* started to develop. A folksonomy is simply a user created method of labeling items so that you or anyone else in your circle of friends of colleagues can use these labels to find your items. A couple of examples are Flickr (**http://www.flickr.com/**) for photos and del.icio.us (**http://del.icio.us/**) for Web site bookmarks. The labels or "tags" used in these sites can be displayed as "clouds" of links to actual data. Here is the way a "tag cloud" displays within such sites (text size indicating relative popularity of the various tags).

ny newyork **nyc** newyorkcity

Simply click on the tag you want, and you will get a display of items that have had that tag attached to them. With these tags (which together form folksonomies), users can search across one another's collections, pulling out, for example, favorite pictures from Japan or bookmarks to sites on ballroom dancing.

One big problem, though: The tags are user generated. This means that consistency goes out the window. One user tags his photos of New York with the term "newyork." Another uses "nyc," or "newyorkcity" or "ny" (most tagging systems demand that you tag with only one word or close up spaces). This means that if I search across the collection for pictures of New York, I need to know all the relevant tags that are being used for the subject, or I will most certainly miss a lot of items just because I didn't use all the right tags.

In some ways, it would be great if some dictator webmaster actually issued a set of standardized tags and insisted that everyone use them instead of making up their own. Hmmm … Actually that's the answer. A set of tags that is uniform so that all the pictures of Japan have to be tagged "JapanPictures," not "JapaneseVacationPictures," or "PicturesOfJapan." That way, you would get all the pictures of Japan that are in the collection.

Too bad I can't claim credit for the idea. The Library of Congress in 1898 was faced with the prospect of creating a new method of cataloging its large collection. As part of the process, the librarians determined that the only way to be sure all books on a particular topic could be identified was to standardize a system of subject headings (tags?) that would be used in the descriptive record (metadata) related to each book. They created records containing these subject headings along with other metadata (authors, titles, etc.).

4.6 Library of Congress Subject Headings

Earlier I showed you a copy of a database record to one of my books. Now I dare to show it again:

LDR: 00793nam 2200265Ia 45x0
005: 20030610113341.0
008: 030610s2003 nyua 001 0 eng d

020: $a 0595271960
035: $a ocm52399619
090: $a LB2375 $b .B33 2003
100: 1 $a Badke, William B., $d 1949–
245: 10 $a Beyond the answer sheet: $b academic success for international students/$c William B. Badke.
260: $a New York: $b iUniverse, $c c2003.
300: $a v, 152 p. : $b ill. ; $c 24 cm.
500: $a Includes index.
650: 0 $a Academic achievement.
650: 0 $a Foreign study.
650: 0 $a College student orientation.
650: 0 $a Student adjustment.
650: 0 $a College students.
650: 0 $a Students, Foreign $x Education (Higher)

If you look at the 650 fields just above, you will see terminology like:

Academic achievement.
Foreign study.
College student orientation.
Student adjustment.
College students.
Students, Foreign $x Education (Higher)

Each of these is a Library of Congress subject heading related to some aspect of the book's subject matter.

How did these subject headings originate? Quite simply, the Library of Congress (LC) in Washington, DC predetermined the terms by which most topics in the world of information would be called and then organized these terms in alphabetical lists. Some subject headings were easy: dogs are **DOGS**, sunflowers are **SUNFLOWERS**, and so on. Some were more difficult: What do you call senior citizens? LC chose **AGED**, much to the outrage of senior citizens. Television faith healers are **HEALERS IN MASS MEDIA**. Why? *Because LC said so.* That's the point with controlled vocabularies. These vocabularies are created by people "out there" who then *control* them and refuse to allow you to change them.

The fact is that you can't have it both ways. You can either choose your own search terminology (as in keywords or tagging), in which case you can't be sure you'll find everything, or you can use standardized terminology not chosen by you. If you use standardized terminology, you have less flexibility, but you are more likely to find most of what the database has to offer about the topic you are seeking. Thus:

Rule #1: *With controlled vocabularies, you have to use the subject terms provided by the system. You might not like the terms chosen, but they are what you've got. No variations are allowed; you have to use the subject headings in the forms provided to you.*

How does a controlled vocabulary work? Armed with a set of predetermined subject headings, catalogers (creators of metadata records) decide which heading (or headings) to assign to a particular chunk of data. In the case of LC, every time they get a book to catalog, they write a description of the book (i.e., the catalog record), which then becomes metadata, and to that metadata is added one or more controlled subject headings.

So a book entitled *Them TV Preachers* may have the subject heading HEALERS IN MASS MEDIA assigned to it. A book called *Active Seniors in Today's World* may be labeled with the subject heading AGED.

Note something very important here. The book *Them TV Preachers* did not have any of the actual words of the subject heading in its title. The title told you the book was about TV preachers. It said nothing about healers or about mass media. The same was true for the second title—*Active Seniors in Today's World*—the term "AGED" is not to be seen anywhere in the title. Why, then, were they given the subject headings they received? *Because some intelligent librarian sat down with these books, determined what they were about, and then assigned the closest subject headings from the already existing controlled vocabulary list.* Thus:

Rule #2: *The actual wording in a title of whatever you are searching for is not important for controlled vocabularies. Subject headings are assigned on the basis of somebody's judgment as to what the item is actually about. The title words can be the same as words in the subject heading or radically different.*

Consider the advantages: I have 5 books with the following titles:

Terminal Choices
Choosing Life or Death
Euthanasia
The Practice of Death
The Right to Die

All of them are about mercy killing or euthanasia. You might not have guessed that fact by looking at the titles, but the intelligent LC librarian has looked over these books, determined that they are all about the same topic, and assigned the same subject heading to all of them: EUTHANASIA.

Controlled vocabularies are a good solution to the problem of *retrieval*. How can we ask the right question so that the database will deliver to us the information we need? If we wanted a list of books about euthanasia, it would be nice to have a search tool that would enable us simply to type a predetermined word or phrase into the computer and get back a list of all the euthanasia books regardless of the wordings of the actual book titles. This is what a *controlled vocabulary* is designed for. Most of the books on euthanasia in a library will be retrieved just by typing in the subject term EUTHANASIA.

Rule #3: *Use a controlled vocabulary as a search tool when you want a collection of data on the same subject regardless of what the data actually says about itself.*

But let's be clear about one thing—controlled vocabularies are "controlled" in the sense that someone other than you has determined what they will be. You as the user can't mess with them by changing their words or rearranging their structure the way you can with keywords. You *use* controlled vocabularies; you don't create them and you can't fool with their form.

Rule #4: *Messing with controlled vocabulary wording or form is strictly forbidden. Subject headings are created by someone other than you, and they can't, in most cases, be manipulated or turned into keywords.*

Let's see how the *LC Subject Headings* controlled vocabulary system works in practice. The Library of Congress provides subject headings for its own books, but it has also conveniently issued its list of approved headings so that all of us can use their system. Most libraries in North America have chosen to do just that, so that your library's subject headings are likely derived from the Library of Congress.

Your library may have a print edition of *Library of Congress Subject Headings* as a set of large red volumes. Below is a mock-up of what you might see on typical page from the guide. On the right are the subject headings or alternative headings. On the left is a description of what you are seeing on the right. If you have trouble distinguishing left from right, look for italics (left) or non-italics (right):

```
LC authorized subject heading (bold print)  -->      Peanuts
                                           [QK495.L52 (Botany)]
Library of Congress Class numbers for peanuts   -> [SB351.P3 (Culture)]
                                      UF  Arachides
     UF = "use for". These are terms        Arachis hypogea
     which LC does not use or authorize.     Earth nuts
     If you looked up "Earth nuts" in LC     Goobers
     Subject Headings, it would say:         Grass nuts
     USE Peanuts.                            Ground-nuts
                                             Groundnuts
     (Bet you never knew peanuts could       Monkey nuts
     called so many things. "Goobers?")      Pindars
                                             Pindas
                                             Pinders

     BT = "broader term." Peanuts        BT  Arachis
     are a subdivision of these.             Oilseed plants
     RT = "related term"                 RT  Cookery (Peanuts)
     NT = "narrower term"                NT  Peanut products
                                         -- Breeding
     These are subdivisions of           -- Irrigation
     "peanuts." There's even one         -- Law and legislation
     subdivision of a subdivision:       -- Storage
     Peanuts -- Storage -- Diseases            -- -- Diseases and injuries
         and injuries.
```

The Library of Congress has also provided a free version of its subject heading system online (**http://authorities.loc.gov/**). While not as extensive as the print edition, it can be a handy way to identify an authorized subject heading. Here's how it works (with the usual disclaimer that everything may be utterly different by the time you read this):

Click on "Search Authorities." On the next screen, make sure you have "Subject Authority Headings" selected, then type in what you think the subject heading should be. For example, you might type in "mercy killing." When you click on "Begin Search," the next screen will give you a list with maroon colored buttons on the left. If the button opposite the term you searched says, "Authorized Heading," then you know you've identified a proper subject heading. If it says "References," it's not an authorized heading, but clicking on the button will tell you what the proper heading is.

NOTE—*this index is not a library catalog in itself.* It is simply a computerized guide to subject headings that you can then take to a catalog and use to find the books you need.

4.7 Working the Angles—Identifying Controlled Vocabularies

Controlled vocabularies can involve more than subject headings. Names can be tricky in databases—Am I "Badke, William" or "Badke, Bill?" Thus many databases also have controlled vocabularies of names, by which they standardize the form of an author's name so you can find everything by that author in the database. Titles of books or articles have their own controlled vocabulary built in. A title takes a unique form in its choice and order of words so that titles tend to be standardized automatically.

But subject headings, whether they are in a library catalog or some other database, are a challenge to identify. Let's look at types of databases that have controlled vocabularies and try to understand how they are organized to provide you information.

4.7.1 Library Catalogs

Library catalogs often do not have guides to subject headings embedded in them, which is why you have to use the *Library of Congress Subject Headings* volumes or the online version, described above. But there is another way to identify subject headings. As a purist, I hesitate to tell you this, because it's not foolproof, and you may end up missing headings you could have used. But here it is: *Starting with a keyword search in a library catalog may be the best way to find relevant subject headings.*

Here's how it works. First do a keyword search in the library catalog, using words you think might appear in relevant books on the topic you are dealing with. Find a book that is right on topic and click on the title of the citation to it to open up the full catalog record. For example, you might be writing on **Pacific Island societies**, so you use these terms in a keyword search. You discover in your result list the ideal book and open up the full record:

The growth and collapse of Pacific island societies: archaeological and demographic perspectives/
Author: Kirch, Patrick Vinton
          Rallu, Jean-Louis
Publisher: Honolulu: University of Hawaii Press, ©2007.
ISBN: 9780824831349

Subjects: Ethnology—Oceania.
          Ethnology—Hawaii.

Look at the line that says "Subjects." There are a couple of official, authorized forms of the Library of Congress subject heading for this concept **Ethnology—Oceania** and **Ethnology—Hawaii**. They may not be the subject headings you would have thought of, but that doesn't matter. What you have with these subject headings are tools to find all the other books on the topic, usually just by clicking on the hyperlinked subject headings in the catalog record.

So this method is relatively simple: Use a keyword search to find one book on your topic. Open up the citation to get the full catalog record. Identify the LC subject heading(s) used for this book and click on its (their) link(s) to search for other books like the first one.

4.7.2 Other Databases

There are a many databases out there that use controlled vocabularies. Here are some clues to finding their subject headings systems:

> A term commonly used is "Thesaurus," that is, a guide to subject headings that not only identifies authorized subjects but also can lead you to broader, narrower or related terms that are also authorized. Sometimes there is a "scope note," that is a definition of what is covered by a certain subject heading.

> At other times in a database you may see a link to "Subjects" or "Descriptors," which mean the same thing.

> In connection with the options above, or sometimes separate from them, you may find a "browse" function. "Browse" generally involves working with controlled vocabulary terms (subjects, authors, titles, etc.) from alphabetized lists of headings.

4.8 Getting Fancy—Combining Controlled Vocabulary and Keyword Searching

Let me begin this section by making something very clear: Keywords and controlled vocabularies are *not the same*. Keywords are constructed by you as best guesses. Controlled vocabularies are constructed by someone else, and their form/order/terminology cannot be changed.

That said, there is a way to construct searches in which a subject heading gets you to the right subject matter, and keywords help you to narrow within that subject area. It's called *faceted searching*. Let's try an example. Consider the following:

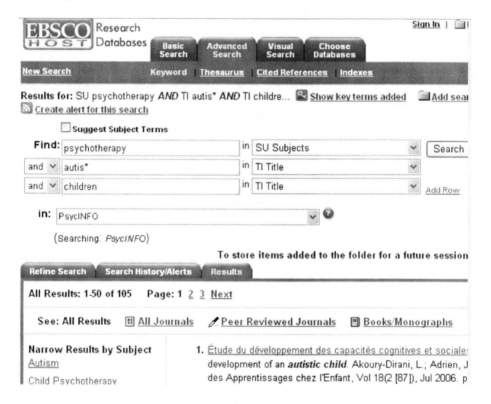

This is an EBSCO journal database entitled PsycINFO, which has a Thesaurus link on bar near the top of the screen. With the thesaurus, I identified an authorized subject heading (descriptor): **Psychotherapy.** That became the subject pool within which I intended to operate. My particular interest was not in every form of psychotherapy but in psychotherapy with autistic children. Thus I began with my subject term "psychotherapy" and added, using an AND search, two title words—**autis*** (truncation for autism, autistic, etc.) and **children.** Rather than getting thousands of titles, many of which are irrelevant, I got 105 relevant citations to journal articles.

In a faceted search, you should most often start the process with a subject heading that finds you most everything on a topic, if you know what the subject heading is. [If not, start with a keyword search, open up the record for one of your results, and identify a subject heading.]

Then add narrowing keywords in an AND search to focus down within that subject area to the particular emphasis you want to make.

Take note that some databases do not allow the combining of subject headings and keywords in a single search, so this approach will not always bear fruit.

4.9 Keeping on Track with Controlled Vocabularies

Many databases today, including most of what is found in a Google search, can be searched only by keyword. Keywords have distinct advantages, but the lack of controlled vocabulary search options can be a definite drawback when all you want is a set of data on one subject regardless of what the data says about itself. Thinking of all possible keywords that might give you relevant data can really give you a headache.

Some people have a lot of trouble grasping the essential difference between keywords and controlled vocabularies, especially when the same words can sometimes be used for both. For example, there is a subject heading **Tax evasion,** but that could just as easily be a keyword form. What's the difference? Well, the keyword search **tax evasion** could bring you up a book like *The Detection of Tax Evasion in the Bronx*. A subject heading search would bring up this title, but it would also find *The Psychology of Escaping the Taxman*, something your keyword search on "tax evasion" would miss completely. What's the difference? Essentially it's in the way the database search engine searches for the words. **Tax evasion** as a keyword search will look only for those actual words in a title. **Tax evasion** as a subject heading will search for all the database records that have been tagged with the subject "TAX EVASION," even if their title words don't contain "tax evasion." With subject headings, results on a subject will come up even if the title words aren't right.

Keywords are best used if you don't know a subject heading or if your topic is narrow or crosses disciplines (like "The education of homeless children"). Controlled vocabulary subject headings are best when you want to find most of what a database has on a subject area, and you are concerned that a keyword search will only reveal some of what is there.

In some situations you can combine the two in a faceted search, using the subject heading to get you into the right subject territory and an additional keyword or two to narrow down within that subject to some aspect of it.

4.10 For Further Study

Study Guide

1. What are "controlled vocabularies", and what is the most familiar example?
2. How are controlled vocabularies created?
3. Why doesn't the actual title of the book matter a great deal when a cataloger attaches a controlled vocabulary term to it?
4. What are the advantages of controlled vocabularies?
5. In Library of Congress Subject Headings, what do the following abbreviations mean?
   UF
   BT
   RT
   NT
6. Explain the method of starting with a keyword search in order to identify controlled vocabulary subject headings.
7. Define the following:
   Thesaurus
   Descriptor
   Browse function
8. Is it possible to search controlled vocabularies and keywords at the same time? When would you want to do so, if it is possible?

Practice with Controlled Vocabularies

1. Use Library of Congress Subject Headings to find the authorized subject heading for the following:
   a. LASH ships
   b. Zen arts
   c. Clothes hangers
   d. Means used to prevent criminal activity
   e. Canadian Religious Poetry

    f.   Books on being a catcher in baseball
    g. Books on how to write for people who are newly literate
    h. Pencilflowers
    i.   The philosophy of Spiritualism
    j.   The Roman influences on law in the United States

2.   In the following catalog record, which are controlled vocabulary terms?

    Title: The hitchhiker's guide to the meaning of everything/William Badke.
    Author: Badke, William B., 1949–
    Publisher: Grand Rapids, MI: Kregel Publications, 2005.
    Description: 176 p. ; 22 cm.
    ISBN: 0825420695
    Subjects: Bible—Criticism, interpretation, etc
           Meaning (Philosophy)—Religious aspects—Christianity.
           Life—Religious aspects—Christianity

Suggested Key to Practice with Controlled Vocabularies

1.   Library of Congress Subject Headings—Correct Headings
    a.   *LASH ships*: USE: Barge-carrying ships
    b.   *Zen arts*: USE: Arts, Zen
    c.   *Clothes hangers*: USE: Coat hangers
    d.   *Means used to prevent criminal activity*: USE: Crime prevention [this one actually made you have to think—sorry].
    e.   *Canadian Religious Poetry*: USE: Religious poetry, Canadian
    f.   *Books on being a catcher in baseball*: USE: Catching (Baseball) or Catchers (Baseball) [made you think again, sorry.]
    g. *Books on how to write for people who are newly literate*: USE: New literates, Writing for [by now, thinking must seem almost normal}
    h. *Pencilflowers* USE: Stylosanthes
    i.   *The philosophy of Spiritualism*: USE: Spiritualism (Philosophy)
    j.   *The Roman influences on law in the United States*: USE: Law United States Roman influences

2.   Clearly the three subject headings are controlled vocabularies: Bible—Criticism, interpretation, etc.; Meaning (Philosophy)—Religious aspects—Christianity; Life—Religious aspects—Christianity. But so is the author (because it is pre-formatted for standardization) and even the title.

Assignment for a Research Project of your Own

Do a *Library of Congress Subject Heading* search for a topic of your choice in a library catalog by:

1. Identifying the best subject heading either through the Library of Congress Subject Headings resource (print or online) or by starting with a keyword search to find a book on the topic and then locating the subject heading you want through that book's catalog record.
2. Do the search by using the appropriate search box for subject headings or by clicking on the relevant link in a catalog record.
3. Carefully evaluate your results to identify those books most relevant to your topic area.
4. Make a list of 8 to 10 relevant books identified through your controlled vocabulary search.

5

Library Catalogs and
Journal Databases

Now we move into the area where the rubber meets the road.

This chapter is intended to guide you through the major database resources available to you in a library, using the keyword and controlled vocabulary methods described in the previous two chapters. Let's start with books:

5.1 Library Catalogs

Books tend to create fogs of misunderstanding, because they're blunt instruments. In order to write a book, you need a topic broad enough to be covered in a couple of hundred or more pages, but you need enough focus to avoid it becoming multi-volume or looking superficial. Thus finding a book specifically on your narrowed down topic may well be a challenge. If you can't find a book on Abortion, you might find one on Medical Ethics. If you can't find a book on Constantine, you might find a book on Roman Emperors or Roman History of his era or Early Church History. Generally, you need to assume that few books will be exactly on your topic. That is why strategies are needed.

Library catalogs have been around forever, it seems, though electronic versions of them have been widely used only over the past twenty-five or so years. When you search a library catalog, you are searching the data record created for each book, a record that includes the following, among other things: Author, title, publisher information, format, description, subject heading(s), and call number. This is where it can get tricky. Library catalog searching interfaces differ widely from one another, so you need to "read" them in order to navigate them well. Some common interface formats:

> ➢ A catalog that offers an initial keyword search box and an advanced search link so you can move to a more sophisticated search screen.

> ➢ A catalog that allows you to specify (through a drop-down, a list, or a choice of buttons) what type of search you want to do (e.g., keyword, title, subject heading, etc.).

> ➢ A catalog that defaults to an advanced search with several boxes that enable you to specify type of search and then shape it with Boolean operators. In this case, a basic search link will be available as well.

Here is a three-part collage of various types of catalog you may encounter:

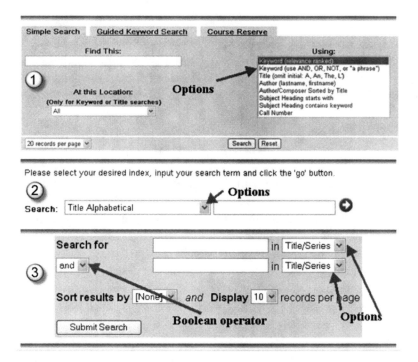

5.1.1 Making the Catalog Work for You

If your topic is reasonably standard, you will probably do best with a controlled vocabulary subject heading search. It's safer in that you know you will find most books that are available on the topic. One problem, beyond sometimes finding too many books to deal with, is that you may only need a portion of the information found in each book. For example, if your research question is, "How close to attainability is B.F. Skinner's utopian vision found in his book *Walden Two?*" you might well find that there are few books available specifically on *Walden Two*, and you are going to have to do a controlled vocabulary subject search on **Skinner, B.F. (Burrhus Frederic), 1904**—and then find material on *Walden Two* within books describing his thought. Of course, you'll also need to look at *Walden Two* itself.

NOTE: For information on how to identify Library of Congress Subject Headings for your search, see Chapter 4.

If your topic is not a standard one or if it combines a couple of subject disciplines (such as the influence of *Walden Two* on the 1960's hippy movement), you may want to go for a keyword approach. Here are a few warnings, however:

> Keywords tend to target specific and/or non-traditional approaches to topics. The library you are using may not have enough diversity to meet your particular quirky need.

> Keyword searching, while it may narrow down your quest to exactly what you want, is a very inexact science. You have to input the right word(s) configured in the right way, and you are highly dependent on the actual terminology of titles in the collection.

> Be sure you don't use too many keywords at once. Start with one or two, and if that doesn't give you what you want, try one more. Rarely, unless you are nesting ANDs and ORs, will you need more than three.

> Never forget that, in an AND search, every time you add a term you eliminate data from your results. This may be good if you have too many hits, but make sure that the data you are eliminating is not crucial. It's better to have more results and have to sift through them to find what you need than to have a smaller set of results that doesn't meet your requirements.

Some catalogs will let you combine controlled vocabulary and keyword searching. If you can do this, you'll need to keep your wits about you. In general, the subject heading gets you into the right territory, the broad subject area.

You add keywords to specify, within this subject area, the narrower concept you are looking for. For example, your subject area might be **Homelessness**. You could then add the keyword, **Canad*** (for **Canada, Canada's, Canadian**, etc.).

Why not, then, simply make them both keywords? Because "homelessness" can be expressed in a variety of ways. In the catalog you might have titles such as:

Canada's Homeless: An Inquiry
Street Life in a Canadian City
Ain't Got No Place to Call My Own: A Canadian's Story

Two of them don't even use the term **homeless.** Thus, using a subject heading that is not dependent on title terminology can gather all the books generally on the subject, and additional keywords will specify which books you want from that broader pool.

Alternatively, you can combine two or more subject headings, looking for where they overlap, though this method is less likely to get you solid results than subject heading and keyword combinations.

Above all in catalog searching, use lateral thinking. Thinking hierarchically could help you. Ask yourself one or more of the following questions:

➢ What hierarchy (broader subject area) or hierarchies could this topic be a part of?

➢ If I can't find a book specifically on my topic, what topic is next above it in the hierarchy?

➢ If one approach is not working, what are other ways that I might look at the topic? (i.e., what other hierarchies could potentially contain the topic?)

5.1.2 E-Books

Electronic books have struggled to catch on as consumer-friendly products. Most people have little desire to sit in front of a screen and read 300 pages of text. Our eyes are too precious to us. True, technological advances, like the Sony Reader and Amazon Kindle that use eye-friendly E Ink, may make a difference for the future, but over the past few years the advances in e-book use have been less than encouraging. A number of commercial e-libraries are available, from NetLibrary and ebrary (that operate mainly through existing library catalogs) to Questia (available by individual subscription) though none of these even approach the size you would find in the print collection of a very small college.

Library catalogs are increasingly linking directly to e-books, though in some cases you will need to search through a separate e-book link. A tip here is to find the broadest keyword search function in the catalog, then use a keyword or two related to your topic but add the AND search term "electronic."

Several Internet-based companies have begun offering e-books or portions of them through their own search engines. The Google Book project (http://books.google.com/) has contracted with major libraries around the world to digitize hundreds of thousands of volumes. Copyright, of course, is an issue, so you can only view a few pages of books that are still under copyright. The real advantage may be for older primary source materials, such as those found in the Oxford University Bodleian Library.

Amazon.com, the bookseller, has a "search within the book" feature that provides access to portions of a lot of books they sell. Their separate search engine A9 Open Search (http://a9.com/-/home.jsp) allows you to search by keyword through many of the books amazon sells, though in most cases you can only view a portion of them.

Not to be outdone, Microsoft has introduced its Windows Live Search Book Publisher Program (http://publisher.live.com/) which will allow searching of book text from contributing publishers, though copyright limitations will still be in effect. The British Library, for example, is digitizing all of its Nineteenth Century titles for inclusion in the Windows Live book program.

Meanwhile, on a less commercial front, the Open Content Alliance (http://www.opencontentalliance.org/) is quietly snagging key contracts with major libraries and library systems that are uncomfortable with Google and Microsoft. Why are libraries uncomfortable? Because the commercial digitizers are intent on keeping control over their content, which can only be read with their software within their systems. OCA intends to make its digital texts more widely available.

As of the end of 2007, the Universal Digital Library (http://www.ulib.org/), another non-commercial project, with backing from the National Science Foundation and other groups, had 1.5 million book titles digitized. Items not in copyright are available in HTML, TIFF and a type of PDF format. Those under copyright offer only an abstract. A significant feature of this collection is the number of Chinese, Arabic and Indian language titles in it. The Online Books Page (http://digital.library.upenn.edu/books/) offers over 25,000 books for free, though most are out of copyright and thus old. The Oxford Text Archive (http://ota.ahds.ac.uk/) offers over 2000 carefully chosen books important to academic study. One of the largest enterprises offering free e-books is Project Gutenberg (**http://www.gutenberg.org/wiki/Main_Page**) which has 20,000 titles of its own and offers 100,000 titles through its affiliates.

What about the grand myth that everything will one day be online for anyone to read? Well, I think you can put that one to rest alongside the story of the baby alligators, earlier dumped into the sewers of New York, that have become twenty foot student-eating monsters. Even if all the books in the world were digitized, the full text of anything in copyright would only come to you at a cost. Authors like to get paid, and well they should, because they are all wonderful people who deserve it. Thus it is futile to believe that any book you want to have can be accessed electronically for free. Publishers don't want to give away their books any more than music producers want to give away their songs (though book piracy may one day make a liar out of me). As well, many older books are not commercially viable for digitization unless they end up in a project like Google Book.

Even with all these efforts, though, the e-book is still finding its way. Don't expect that everything you need will soon be available to you electronically at home in the middle of the night while you're munching on a pickle and desperately trying to finish that research project before the doom of morning strikes.

5.2 Journal Databases

Just when you thought that finding books was trouble enough, someone is sure to suggest to you that there's another whole world of research materials crying out for attention—*journals*. Actually, the whole category I'm thinking of is broader than that. Librarians, ever the stuffy folks we are, call them "periodicals," that is, materials that arrive in the library periodically, as opposed to a book that arrives only once. Included in the category is everything from newspapers to popular magazines (or e-zines) to scholarly journals. But I'm going to call them journals anyway, because the primary readers of this book are doing academic research that focuses on journals.

5.2.1 Some Background on the Journal Scene.

Before we get to journal databases, let's clarify what makes journals different from books. The most significant difference is that you can't catalog a journal like you catalog a book. When a librarian gets a new book for the collection, the book is cataloged (i.e. has a catalog record created for it) and put on the shelf. After that, there is nothing to do but sign the book out and check it back in until it falls apart. The cataloger's job is done.

But journal issues *keep on arriving* every week or month or quarter or year. By definition, they are *periodical*. You can't just create a descriptive record for them once and for all like you can a book, because they keep changing as more issues are added to the growing collection. While it might be possible for a librarian to assign a subject heading to each article in each journal as it arrives and then to create a database so that you could find articles on any given topic, it just wouldn't be practical. No librarian has the time to create a separate database of all the library's journal articles.

The field of journals is governed by several categories, some of which are showing rapid change:

Popular vs. Scholarly

Popular magazines generally come from a different mindset than do scholarly journals. Both are supposed to inform, but popular magazines also need to some degree to entertain. Their audiences are different, with scholarly journals being the territory of scholars and students in higher education. In the middle are *trade magazines* that tend to specialize in some particular industry or technology where information is shared. They are less "popular" in tone but generally look like popular magazines and do not have a lot of footnotes or bibliographies.

The scholarly world uses a system of *peer review*, by which manuscripts submitted for possible publication are read by other scholars in the field (peers) as a gatekeeping process intended to weed out inferior work. Peer review itself has come under attack as preserving the status quo and preventing younger scholars with fresh ideas from publishing, but it is still the best system we've got.

Print vs. Electronic

Over the past decade or more, journals have been moving dramatically into the electronic world. Most published journals now have both print and electronic versions available. Some are only electronic. In fact, I suspect that the print journal will soon become a rarity, saving thousands of trees and the squirrels that inhabit them. Why? Simply because people really like what e-journals can do for them. E-journals are instantly accessible from anywhere that has Internet access, you can print only what you want to keep, and they are much more searchable for key concepts within articles than are print journals.

But there are issues. To tell the truth about electronic journals:

> ➤ They are still somewhat limited. Some journals are simply not available electronically. Others do have an electronic life, but your library may not have access to them.

> ➤ Back-runs in electronic form are generally short, going back into the 1990s but rarely earlier.

> ➤ Format can be a challenge—HTML loads faster in your computer but sometimes doesn't contain original graphics and loses the original page numbers. PDF has graphics and the original page numbers but loads more slowly and creates a larger file than does HTML. PDF is increasingly the format of choice for most online journals.

Many students are tempted to consider only journal articles that are available in full text, bypassing citations to articles the library may have in print or microform. That can be a mistake if the best article on a topic is only available in some hardcopy format. It's wise to avoid taking the easy road just so you can finish your research early. (Why do I sense you're resisting what I'm telling you? Really. It's true—good, thorough research might demand using the occasional print journal or even microfiche, but this is far more satisfying than simply getting the job done fast so you can go to a movie).

Pay vs. Open Access

The pay/open access distinction may not mean much to you if you are a student in higher education, because your institution provides the journals as part of those incredibly high tuition fees you pay. But unrestricted access to even more journals will increase over the next couple of decades due to the open access movement.

Here's what's happening: As journal subscriptions increase in price, it's occurring to universities that they are often paying for their journals twice. First, their own professors get research grants from public funding bodies to write the articles. Then, when the articles are published, universities, funded by public money, have to pay high subscription fees to get access to the same articles already funded from the same public purse. It's as if the government paid for the research twice and only the journal publishers walked away with profits.

So increasingly, research grants come with a restriction—if you are going to publish an article at the end of the research grant process, within 6 months or so that article has to be made public online.

As newer journals come into existence, their producers are increasingly making them open access from the beginning—free, online and available.

These journals still use peer review and maintain quality, but anyone can read them without a subscription.

For searchable databases of open access journals, go to Open J-Gate (**http://www.openj-gate.com/**) or Directory of Open-Access Journals (**http://www.doaj.org/**).

5.2.2 Introduction to Journal Databases

Even thinking of using journals in a research project may produce in you a shudder of horror. You imagine sitting down in front of piles of printed journals, thumbing through each one in an anguished quest for something (anything!) on the "The Implications for Generation Y of Max Weber's Approach to the Sociology of Cities." Hours later, in bitterness of heart and soul, you will emerge, red-eyed, with one article that is only vaguely relevant.

Journal research used to be done that way when your grandfather was a wee lad in school. Now things are very different, due to the development of journal databases.

These databases are created this way: Indexers sit down in front of piles of print journals or their electronic equivalents (often related to a specific subject discipline, such as psychology or history or religion) and create a metadata record for each article. The metadata is loaded into the database, thus making it searchable. By doing a search, you can generate a list of articles from various journals that are relevant to the subject you are studying.

Approaching a journal database means first being able to "read" its *interface*. The interface is what you actually see on the computer screen when you search for the data in a journal database. It includes the screen display, search methods, and so on. Interfaces change constantly. Data doesn't. What this means is that the screen may look different the next time you use the database. The instructions on use may be different. Even the methods you need to follow to search the index may be different. The data inside the database is the same, but the means you use to extract it may be brand new.

How to Read an Interface

➢ *Go over any instructions on the screen.* Look, as well, for anything that says "search tips" or "how to use this index," etc.

➢ Start with a keyword search and identify 2 or 3 results that look like they are relevant to your research question/thesis.

➢ Click on the titles of these relevant articles, one by one, to open the full records. Are the authors' names hyperlinked (pointing to a controlled vocabulary of names so that no matter what form an author's name takes, all that author's articles on the topic are accessible under one standardized name form)? Are there subject headings? Do the headings seem specific or are they very broad in their coverage?

➢ Are there suggested subject heading links beside or above the list of results? Are they hyperlinked? If so, they may help you to take your keyword(s) into the right subject area. For example, if you may have initially done a keyword search on "globalization" and one of the suggested subject headings next to the results is "social justice," then you can focus your emphasis down to social justice issues in globalization.

➢ Look for a "Thesaurus," "Subjects," "Browse Subjects," or "Indexes" link. Any of these can take you to authorized subject headings for this database. In this case, you can start with one subject area, then either link it to another subject area or to one or more keywords in an AND search.

➢ If you are going to search by keywords, what sorts of Boolean operators are in use in this database? Is phrase searching allowed?

➢ Try a search on a broad basis first, perhaps inputting a subject heading or only one keyword. If you get more than about 500 "hits" (citations to individual articles), look for a means to refine or arrow your search by adding more words. But be careful, in doing so, not to eliminate good data—it's better to have more hits than to miss crucial articles because you narrowed with too much vigor.

Let's start with an example

If you want to learn to swim in the shark-infested waters of journal database searching, you have to arm yourself and just jump in. Let's look at a sample search using *EBSCO Academic Search Premier*, a user-friendly database with considerable full text content. By the time you read this, the interface may have changed, but the image below gives you a good idea of ways in which sophisticated databases can do a good job of leading you to relevant journals.

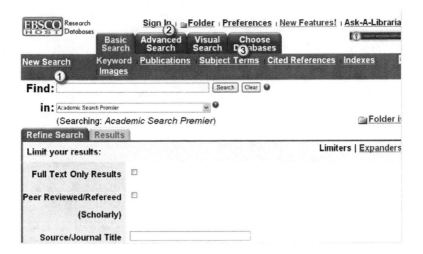

[My thanks to EBSCO for permission to use screenshots of its databases.]

Notice some of the features of this first screen, coded by number:

1. There is a box that allows you to enter information (**Find**).

2. While this is a "basic search," you can also do an "advanced search" that allows you to build your investigation using Boolean terms.

3. There is also a "Subject Terms" button, indicating that this index has a controlled vocabulary. In some databases, this will be called "Thesaurus." To help you identify the right subject heading, there will be a "browse" function that opens up when you click on "subject heading" or "thesaurus." Type in what you think the subject heading is, and you will be taken to the place in the list of subject headings where that term will be found. Generally, you can then click on the heading or put a check mark in a box to search that subject heading.

This is what a "browse" screen looks like:

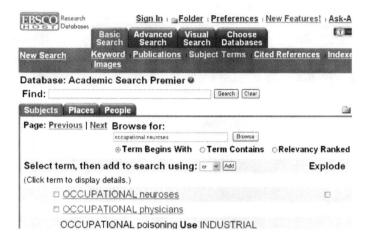

Notice that I have browsed for **occupational neuroses** (one of which I'm sure I've acquired), and I've produced an alphabetical list of subject headings, the first of which is the one I want. Clicking on the checkbox and then on "Add" (to add it to my search) will enable me to find all the articles in the database on this topic.

Now let's have a look at the limiters and expanders, which are commonly found on most types of journal database, though the numbers and types of them will vary from database to database. Limiters and expanders simply narrow or broaden your search.

1. You can limit to full text articles only, but never forget that the best article for your topic may not be in full text, so turning on this limiter could eliminate a valuable resource. Most databases have citations to many more journal articles than are actually provided in full text.

2. You can limit to scholarly articles only (peer review refers to a process by which manuscripts submitted to a journal are checked out by experts in the field, who determine whether or not it will be published—a great process for the journal, but nasty for the author of the manuscript, as my own scars will show).

3. You can limit by specifying a certain journal.

4. You can limit to a certain date range, but you may not have to, because most databases sort the found articles by most recent first.

5. You can choose the type of publication you are looking for, limit to articles that are longer or shorter in number of pages, even choose only certain formats for images within articles.

6. You can expand (broaden) your search by searching for additional terms (those with other endings, such as "s", "ed," and so on).

5.2.3 Some Tips on Journal Article Citations

A journal article citation is simply a description of an article with sufficient information to help you find it. While the format of a citation may vary, this is the information usually provided:

Badke, William. "Can't Get No Respect: Helping Faculty to Understand the Educational Power of Information Literacy." *The Reference Librarian* 43, no. 89/90 (2005): 63-80.

Here it is broken down:

Badke, William.—Author of the article.

"Can't Get No Respect: Helping Faculty to Understand the Educational Power of Information Literacy."—Title of the article.

The Reference Librarian—Name of the journal in which the article is found.

43—Volume number of the journal. Each new year gets a new volume number.

no. 89/90—Issue number. In this case, this is a double issue.

(2005)—Date the article was published.

63-80—Page numbers of the issue in which the article is found.

5.2.4 Journal Databases with Electronic Full Text

Rather than simply listing citations to various journal articles, full text databases add the actual text of the articles in electronic form—usually as HTML or PDF or both, the former looking like a re-typed document, and the latter looking like a photocopy of the original print version. Increasingly, journal databases are going to PDF only. You can usually e-mail articles from your library to your home computer if you're not already searching a database remotely from home.

Before you begin believing that all journal literature is now available to you in electronic form whenever you want it, take a reality check. The real world couldn't possibly be that accommodating. While e-journals are coming into their own in a very big way (unlike the lagging e-books), not every article you want will be available to you electronically, though you will likely be able to get most things you need if you open your heart to other formats in your library's collection (print or microform) or to interlibrary loan.

Contrary to the beliefs of some people, most journal articles are not accessible through a Google search. They are found in specialized databases that require passwords for access.

5.3 Approaching Journal Databases— Tips and Hints

5.3.1 Be prepared for frustration.

The journal scene is not nearly as tidy as books are. Journals provide a never-ending supply of issues year after year after year, they can exist in a variety of formats (Internet, computer files, paper, microfilm, microfiche), and chances are the very article you need is nowhere to found in your metropolitan area.

Here's a psychological trick that might help you—*prepare yourself for frustration.* An illustration: If you are aware from long experience that you will face a traffic jam every day on the way to work, you are ready for it. Only when a traffic jam happens unexpectedly, in a spot you didn't expect it, do you get frustrated. In the same way, if you prepare yourself for journal database frustration, you're less likely the mutter to yourself when it happens.

Before you start using a database, say to yourself, "I know this search is going to tax the last fragments of my patience, but it's good for me, it really, really is, and *I will succeed!*"

5.3.2 Read the Interface.

Every journal database is different in the way it searches and the search options it offers, even two databases produced by the same company. Before you simply throw some words at a database and demand articles in return, check out what's available to you. Is there an advanced search? Is there a thesaurus or a subject heading search? In what ways can you limit or expand your search?

5.3.3 Be aware that databases tend to be something of a black hole.

You send in a request, and the database tells you what it found (or didn't find). The database search program will rarely tell you what you did wrong. It won't give you three 6.5's and an 8 like Olympic judges do. The data you want could well be in there, but you won't know that unless you vary your search strategies to draw it out.

5.3.4 Resist the urge to fill the search box with words.

Most keyword searches can be done with two words or, at the most, three. Remember this simple rule—the more you input into the search box the more strain you're putting on your search. If it's an AND search, you are telling the database that you want *only* those articles that have every word you've entered (which often results in zero hits). If it's an OR search, every article that has any one of your words will appear (resulting in thousands of hits sometimes). Get focused. Use as few words as you need to define your topic.

5.3.5 Think about staging (faceting) your search.

Unlike Google, where you do a search and then pull in your results like fish at the end of a line, a journal database allows you the option of starting broadly and then narrowing in stages. "Stages?" you ask, bewildered that I would even suggest that you wouldn't get great results on the first try. Yes, stages. Like a video game requires stages or like most any activity in life requires steps to be taken. In our example of a real search below, I'll show you how to stage (or facet) a search.

5.3.6 Look for controlled vocabularies and advanced searches.

Tools like controlled vocabularies and advanced searches can help you to specify what you want, especially when keywords could be ambiguous. For example, if I searched EBSCO *Academic Search Premier* (a general subject database) for **paranoia**, I would get a host of articles on all kinds of paranoia—political, social, suspicious spouses, people claiming to have been kidnapped by aliens, folks suspicious of luncheon meats, and so on. If I could find a subject heading within *Premier* for the psychological disorder of paranoia (and I could), I would limit the field considerably. Now, if I tried an advanced search—SUBJECT Paranoid Schizophrenia and KEYWORD Fear, I would find articles on the issue of fear among people with a psychotic version of paranoia.

5.3.7 Think before you search.

Even when you figure out how a journal database actually works, you need to think deeply about the terms you input. What will uniquely identify your topic in the minimum number of words? If your results show hit rates of 1,000 to

100,000 articles, you're aiming too broadly in your search, and you need to narrow down your terminology. If you are getting only one or two hits, you've probably gone too narrow by inputting too many search terms or asking for something so minute that there is only one scholar in the whole world who's remotely interested in the topic, and she's on vacation.

5.3.8 Retrace your steps.

Be prepared to go back and figure out what you did wrong or how you could get better results. Look for "Refine Search" or "Search Again" options. Journal database searching often demands experimentation to find just the right combination of terms that will nail down what you are looking for.

5.3.9 When in doubt, read the instructions.

Every journal database worth its salt has instructions to guide you through the process of searching. When you've exhausted your own common sense, read the instructions. Different databases have different capabilities and search techniques. You may find that the reason you get 354,000 hits one time and zero the next is that you are abusing the database by trying to make it do things it's not prepared even to contemplate.

5.3.10 Remain calm.

What's the most terrible thing that could happen if you blew a search? You might have to try again or (worst case scenario) one of your friends will have watched you fail. Rarely will you have done any permanent harm to the database itself (unless you got violent, which is not recommended), so the only damage is to your time and your ego. If you find yourself hopelessly lost, there is usually a reference librarian to help you out. Swallow your pride and ask for help. Having a bad day in front of a database isn't the end of the world. Above all, resist those evil thoughts that take up residence in your mind, such as, "I will never ever get this" or, "For people like me, ignorant would be a step up," "I must be a few pepperoni short of a pizza," or, "I want to break something." Cool your heart and try again.

5.3.11 Sometimes problems arise because you're using the wrong database.

A database for agriculture journals won't help you with a psychology project. A history database won't be much good if you're researching cockroaches. Using the right database for the job is a rule not to be forgotten. If you can't find one for the subject area you're working on, try a larger, broadly based, database that covers a number of different topics. These types of databases, however, have their own problem in that their coverage of any one subject area is limited.

5.3.12 Check out the possibilities of interlibrary loan.

A database may provide a citation to an article you really want, but the electronic full text is not available and the library does not have the article in any other format. Fret not. While not all academic libraries offer interlibrary loan, maybe yours does. Have a look at your library web page for information or ask a librarian. There now, do you feel better?

5.4 Citation Searches, Related Articles and Reference Lists—Alternative Ways of Searching

5.4.1 Citation Searches

In the sciences and to some extent the social sciences, the relative importance of journal articles (and their authors) is measured by the number of citations to them found in other articles or books. If an article is cited often, it is viewed as being more important than if it is seldom or never cited.

What is more, citations of a key target article in other articles or books can form a history of how the target article has been used by other scholars since it was published. Finding out who has cited a key target article can also be a good way to add to your own resources.

The major tool used in citation searching is Web of Knowledge's three part citation index system—Science Citation Index, Social Sciences Citation Index, and Arts and Humanities Citation Index. While fairly complex to use, you can start with a keyword search, get a list of results, and then sort the list by "Times Cited." When you find an oft-cited (sounds Shakespearean, doesn't it?) article, you can click on the "Times Cited" link to get a list of the articles that have cited it. Not only does this tool help you determine the relative importance of articles, but it can get you a whole list of articles that have cited an important one, thus building up your own resources.

5.4.2 Related Articles

A few databases, like PubMed (**http://www.ncbi.nlm.nih.gov/sites/entrez**) offer a link within citation lists for "related articles," or "find more like these." While not common, a feature like this can be of great help when you want to add to resources.

5.4.3 Reference Lists

A number of databases (e.g., EBSCO's version of PscyINFO) provide, right in their citations, a list of all the sources a particular article used in its notes or bibliography. Thus, even if you can't get the article itself, you can discover the books, articles, etc. to which that article referred. Once again, this adds to the number of resources you can identify for your own research.

5.5 A First Adventure with a Real Live Journal Database

Let's test-drive a real journal database, remembering that interfaces and features vary, depending on which one you use. In our case, we will be taking EBSCO's *Academic Search Premier* for a spin around the block.

We are beginning with the controversial question, "To what extent is the US military to blame for the looting and destruction of museums during the Iraq War that began in 2003?"

I can start with a simple keyword search, just to see what's out there. In this case, the terms **Iraq AND museums** should do the trick. (Notice that I'm not searching **Iraq War** but trying to connect Iraq and museums on the assumption that the museum destruction issue will be prominent among results.) I end up with 237 results:

Take note of a couple of key elements:

1. I have a set of results, some of them with links to electronic full text, others with "Check for availability" links, possibly to other databases that have those articles or to other formats.

2. I also have a "narrow results by subject" set of links on the left. This gives me the opportunity to find a particular focus area and perform a next stage search to limit to the articles that are the most relevant. For example, I could limit to IRAQ War, 2003– .

Here's another option: Start with a subject heading search. In this case, we are dealing with a topic that was part of the Iraq War. Academic Search Premier has a "Subject Terms" search that allows you to input "Iraq War" to browse to the right subject heading (IRAQ war, 2003–). Once you have it, you can add **AND Museums** to narrow to that aspect of the Iraq War you're most interested in. Thus you are using a subject heading to get you into the right context and a keyword to specify within that context what you are actually searching for. Have a look at the steps specified by the numbers in the screenshot below:

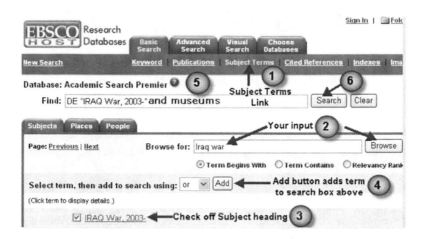

There is an easier way to do this, and that is to start with the results of your first keyword search above. Find a relevant article citation and click on its title to open the full record. If subject headings are available, you can click on one to get you into the right subject area:

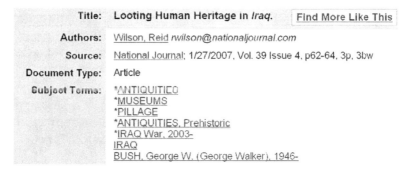

Click on the link for IRAQ War, 2003– , then add as a second stage **and Museums**. The logic here is that you want to start out in the right territory (Iraq War, 2003–), then narrow down to an aspect of that territory (museums). There's no point in finding an article about Iraq museums from 1959, if the looting/destruction happened in 2003. If the Iraq War is the context for this event happening, then starting out with all the articles about the Iraq War gets you into the right territory, and the keyword **museums** narrows to exactly the right topic. In my search, I ended up with 28 highly relevant results instead of the 236 mixed-relevance results I got from just a keyword search on **Iraq museums**.

5.6 Varieties of the Journal Database

At one time, the population of journal search tools tended to be quite stable. You had your *Reader's Guide to Periodical Literature*, and then a whole host of subject discipline specific indexes:

Art Index	*Chemical Abstracts*	*Psychological Abstracts*
Biography Index	*Education Index*	*Philosopher's Index*
Biological Abstracts	*Historical Abstracts*	*Religion Index One*
Business Periodical Index	*Humanities Index*	*Sociological Abstracts*

And so on. The only difference among them, other than subject, was that some offered abstracts (summaries of the articles) as well as citations to articles from various journals and others only had citations.

While some of the older indexes live on in computerized database form, others have changed their names or combined with related databases. There are some that are totally new and attempt to address new demands such as full text capability and faceted searching. It's now virtually impossible to keep up with the types of databases available or with their ever changing interfaces. Staying in touch with research libraries and librarians seems to be the only way to remain up to date. Of course, for many people even the thought of keeping in touch with a librarian is repugnant, despite the fact that we're the nicest people in the world.

If you expect change in this area of research, you won't be disappointed. Despite the fact that it's hard for anyone to keep up, the capabilities of these newer databases are amazing and you can benefit greatly from them as long as you keep your wits about you.

5.7 Federated Search

Federated search is a relatively new option that attempts to deal with the wide variety of databases out there. Essentially, a federated search program gives you a single search box that sends your search out to a number of databases at once and brings the results back into single set of results. It's like harnessing a whole bunch of databases and rounding them up into a single corral. Some federated search programs will give you the option of selecting a subject discipline within which to search (e.g., psychology, biology), thus limiting the number of databases that have to be federated. In many instances, you can draw together a search of the library book catalog and various journal databases available to your library.

This sounds like the wave of the future for research, but before you rejoice too quickly, you should be aware of the limitations of federated search:

> The minute you take even two databases and federate them, you often lose the special search functions of each and are left with a lowest common denominator consisting of only the features those two databases have in common. Add more databases, and pretty soon you are left with a Google-style search box only.

> The more databases you federate, the more results you have to sift through.

> Since federating search engines means losing the search features that help to narrow searches, the results as a whole are much less precise and specifically relevant to your search than what you can find with a single database devoted to your subject area.

I once made the unfortunate statement on an e-mail listserv of several thousand professional librarians that, "Federated search is as dumb as a bag of hammers." Others have described it as a "step above Google." Both may be exaggerations. Federated search does have its uses either when you don't know what specific database you want to search or when you don't want to take the time to search several databases separately. Combining them into one simplified search instrument can be helpful. But remember that federated search is like using a machete to do eye surgery—it may give you results, but they're likely to be uglier than if you'd used a scalpel.

5.8 Final Pep Talk

Don't be afraid of journals and journal databases. They want to be your friends. Scholarly articles in journals and magazines will provide you with a wealth of current and specific information that you dare not ignore. Just heed the following pieces of advice, and you will survive the journal maze:

> Stay calm.

> Stay focused.

> Read the directions.

> ➢ Plan your searches well.

> ➢ Ask for help when you need it.

5.9 For Further Study

Study Guide

1. In a library catalog, when would you use controlled vocabulary subject headings, and when would you use keywords?
2. How can hierarchies help you when you are searching a library catalog for a topic?
3. Why is it futile to believe that the electronic full text of any book you want will be available to you for free?
4. How are journal databases created, and what are they intended to do?
5. Explain the difference between "data" and "interface."
6. Identify each part of the following journal citation:

William Badke, "International Students: Information Literacy or Academic Literacy?" *Academic Exchange Quarterly* 6, no. 4 (Winter 2002): 60-65.

7. In journal database searching you should be prepared for _____. How does such preparation help you?
8. Why should you resist the urge to fill the search box with words?
9. What are the advantages of thinking before you search?
10. Explain the procedure of starting with a subject heading and adding keywords. Why is it often better to stage your searches with subject headings and keywords than simply to do a one-stage keyword search?
11. More and more journals are being offered in electronic "full text" format. What are some of the advantages and difficulties with accessing full text?
12. What are advantages and disadvantages of federated search?

Practice with Journal Databases

Go to one of your institution's databases and "read" the interface, trying to figure out what search features it provides.

Assignment for a Project of Your Own

1. Choose a topic of interest to you.
2. Choose two journal databases. If you do not have access to university databases like those produced by EBSCO, ProQuest, and so on, choose from Internet-based databases: **http://www.ingentaconnect.com/**, **http://www.findarticles.com/**, or **http://magportal.com/** (but note that these databases are not nearly as sophisticated as commercial products available through your library).
3. After having a good look at their interfaces, do a journal search on your topic with each database.
4. Indicate what subject terms or keywords you used in your searches.
5. List 6 articles from each database that are relevant to your topic—author, article title, title of periodical, volume number, date, page numbers.

Note: Be sure the databases you use are relevant to your topic. Not all databases are relevant to any one topic.

6

Internet Research

The early 1990s saw the beginning of an information revolution as dramatic as the invention of the printing press in 1440 (though, typical of our narrow Western mindset, we usually ignore the fact that the Chinese people had a printing press 400 years earlier). The printing press made it possible to replace the normal copying of documents by hand with a process that produced multiple copies in much more rapid succession. All of a sudden, the availability of written information increased dramatically.

The World Wide Web in the 1990s created the same kind of revolution, but on a larger scale. An information delivery system primarily concerned with paper and print (libraries, bookstores, hard copy journal subscriptions and so on) became an electronic universe available to anyone with a computer and a service provider. Today, the average student gets well over two-thirds of his/her information from the Net.

Please supply your own answer to the following question: **The Internet is a world where:** _____

Stumped? Let me supply some possibilities:

The Internet is a world where:

> ➤ you can truly interact with the rest of humanity.

> ➤ you can find information on virtually any topic.

> ➤ almost everyone is trying to sell you something.

> ➤ you can surf until your eyes fall out.

➢ anything that's worth anything costs *money* to retrieve (or else you're told that access is "forbidden!").

➢ you can meet new friends or pick up predators.

➢ you can't trust anyone or any piece of information.

➢ you can get your questions answered.

➢ you can waste a lot of time.

Maybe your response should be "all of the above." The Internet is wonderful and frustrating, helpful and potentially dangerous, beneficial and a waste of time. If keyword searching is the Wild West, the Internet is Dodge City. Why bother with it then? Because it has become the common denominator of our daily lives.

What do I mean? All of us know that most transactions today are becoming digital—we use bank machines and online banking, we use computer library catalogs, we find the Net to be a venue for social interaction, and many of us are shopping from home over the electronic highway. As the phenomenon of doing things electronically grows, the only common medium that can meet its needs is the Internet. The Net has become the basis, the common denominator, for the things we need to get done. It is the number one vehicle for all informational research, whether through a search engine or a specialized subscription database.

True, there are now calls to start over with this thing, using what we have learned to create a new World Wide Web that works more efficiently. But no one is advocating that we abandon the whole idea. Thus we'd better try to understand it.

6.1 A Brief Introduction to the Net

The Internet has been around for a quite awhile, but most people weren't aware of it until the early 90s. Back in the late 1960s, the US military developed a worldwide computer network in order to remain in communication with everybody involved in the space program and defense research. This network (really a network of networks) eventually came into the hands of non-military people—scientists, computer buffs, and so on. It lacked a common communication language that was easy to use, so only specialists could profit from it. In the 1990s, a common communication language and a common communication protocol were established so that anyone who had access to this network could move around it with ease. This resulted in the formation of the World Wide Web.

The following sites on the Internet will provide you with good information about using it for research purposes:

http://www.learnthenet.com/english/index.html
This one, called *Learn the Net*, is very informative and user friendly. It also has a lot of links to other information about the Net.

http://www.lib.berkeley.edu/TeachingLib/Guides/Internet/FindInfo.html
This is a tutorial with links from the University of California, Berkeley.

Disclaimer: In the pages that follow, several Internet URLs will be given. Addresses change rapidly on the Net, so I make no guarantee that you will find what you're seeking by inputting the URLs given. Sorry, but that's life, raw and nasty, though still interesting nevertheless. Keep in touch with the update page for this book: **http://www.acts.twu.ca/lbr/updates.htm.**

6.2 The Language of the Net

Let's consider some terminology:

Browser—a program that gives you access to the Internet and its searching tools as well as allowing you to manipulate and download data. Two common examples are *Internet Explorer* and *Firefox* (or *Safari* for you Mac users).

Home Page—the first screen you come to when you open your browser. It is also the front door or first room in any Internet site.

URL—Uniform Resource Locator, a specific "address" for a database or information site available through the Internet. It's analogous to a telephone number that helps to link your phone with someone else's phone, except that, for an URL, you are linking computers. The typical URL begins with **http://**then has a distinctive alpha-numeric description in which there are no spaces. Thus, you can find the ERIC database if you go to the URL: **http:www.eric.ed.gov**

Search Engine—the World Wide Web is a network of thousands (millions?) of computers linked, essentially, through telephone lines or other cable systems.

Each database held by one of these computers has an "address". But if you don't know a specific address yet you want information on a topic, a "search engine" is what you need. The average search engine asks you to input one or more keywords. The search engine then goes through thousands of networked computer databases (actually through the search engine's own indexed snapshot of the Internet), looking for your keyword(s). You are presented with a list of relevant database sites, with some summary information for each.

More on search engines shortly.

World Wide Web—often described as WWW. It is an organizational system for sites on Internet, allowing a user with a search engine to find information from many databases using a common language (HTML) and a common method of communication (HTTP).

HTML—the common language of the World Wide Web. It stands for *HyperText Markup Language.* This is the language in which data in the World Wide Web is written.

HTTP—*HyperText Transfer Protocol,* a formatting method to determine content and means of transfer of information on the Net. If we were to use the phone system as an analogy, http would be like the method that phone companies worldwide have agreed upon to make sure a phone in Nigeria can communicate with a phone in England. Http is the protocol that is used within the World Wide Web to allow communication among Web sites. Most Internet URLs begin with "http."

Document—on the Net, a document is any collection of information that you locate in your search (home page plus related pages on one Internet site).

Link—a feature of the World Wide Web that allows you to move from one document to another by way of a *hyperlink* or just plain "link." A link in a document is a word or phrase with colored letters, sometimes underlined. With it, you can move from document to document without typing in a lot of addresses.

Bookmark—your browser has a bookmark or "favorites" function that allows you to record the addresses of sites on the Internet that you want to return to. When you want to return, you can click your mouse on that bookmark, and you will be taken to that site without needing to type an address. You can use **http://del.icio.us/**to organize and share bookmarks, if that is your desire.

6.3 Google Scholar and other Free Academic Search Engines on the Net

6.3.1 Free Journals—An Academic Myth

Ah, the ever-hoped-for, ever-elusive dream of being able to access the full text of every journal article you need, right from your computer screen! It could be a reality right now but, alas, reality is never what we hope it will be.

Right now, you can go to a journal database, do a search and get a citation that includes the full text of the article. Click your mouse a few times and you can have the full text of the article either printed out or sent to your own e-mail address. The dream has been fulfilled, and you need never again have to struggle to get your hands on just the right article. Correct?

Well, not exactly. While it is true that many databases provide full text, most of them require a subscription by an institution as well as password protection. As far as genuinely free journal articles are concerned, there are still limitations on the titles and scope of journals available.

Why can't every article from every journal in the world be offered in digital form for minimal or no cost? To answer, let me give you a brief primer on economics. Our world turns on our ability to manufacture things and sell them to other people. If we all worked really hard to produce things and then gave away what we produced, the world would stop spinning on its axis and life as we know it would disappear. Economics makes the world go around.

Thus journal publishers, before they make their material available to vendors of full text databases, demand to be paid and paid handsomely. If the journal publisher cannot (or will not) come to agreement with the database vendor, the full text for that journal will not be available except for a fee on the journal publisher's Web site. Full text is rarely free—it is paid for by your library's expensive subscriptions to journal databases or to individual journals online.

We are now living in an era of serious transition for scholarly journals. Most of them provide electronic versions via the Internet to people who subscribe to the print versions. The next step, over the coming years will be the abandonment of paper subscriptions in favor of electronic full text subscriptions only. The smartest journal publishers are making deals with companies like EBSCO or ProQuest or InfoTrac to provide electronic access within databases. Alternatively, publishers can create their own electronic full text, charge libraries the full subscription price, and EBSCO or some other vendor can include them as a link within one of its databases. Some companies like Sage and Oxford, who have extensive journal holdings, are selling package electronic subscriptions of their own journals (usually with a database search engine) to libraries.

So what's the point of doing all this database searching from library web pages when there are tons of good journals right on the Internet?

Your question reflects that common academic myth—believing that most journal articles are available for free on the Net through a Google search, without password protection.

As we have seen, this is not so.

The production of journal and popular magazine articles is big business in our world. While lots of people put up Web sites at no charge to you, few publishers of journal articles are even remotely as generous (except for those who are part of the open access movement described in Chapter One). The vast majority of journal articles, even those that are electronic, can only be accessed by you or your local university paying a hefty price. Sure, you can find some really good articles for free, but that's not true for most of them. The databases you use through your library may come to you via the Internet, but they are password-protected for a reason—your library has paid big money for subscriptions to them.

But this does not mean that there are no search engines for free academic material on the Net. Let's take a look at some academic tools that provide you with resources that are actually available at no cost through the WWW.

6.3.2 Google Scholar (http://scholar.google.com)

Google Scholar is not really a subset of the Google search engine, but a resource devoted to scholarly literature—books, journal articles, conference proceedings and academic Web sites found on the WWW. Think of it as a type of academic federated database. As such, GS does have its challenges:

> ➢ It is limited to the standard basic search box and some rather elementary advanced search features. Thus any sophisticated search techniques using controlled vocabularies or clustering are out of the question.

> ➢ Not all publishers of academic information are included.

> ➢ It's unclear how results are ordered. What qualifies results to be on the first page as opposed to being on the fifth or twentieth? In GS, there is no way to reorganize the results by date or even by type of material.

Articles, books, conference proceedings and academic Web sites are all jumbled together.

> ➤ The quest for actual full text is a frustrating one. More often than not, following a link to a journal article will get you only to an abstract of it. The full text will cost you significant coin. This can be offset in a couple of ways: by checking to see if your academic library has linked its journal holdings to GS (see **http://scholar.google.com/intl/en/scholar/ librarylinks.html**) or by checking your own library's journal list to see if it subscribes to the journal you want.

All of that said, Google Scholar can be a very useful tool, especially for helping to identify a resource about which you have only partial information, for finding other articles by an important author on your topic, or simply as one more place to search for resources. It will not, however, usually serve as a good substitute for journal databases available through your library.

The Scholar help screens (**http://scholar.google.com/intl/en/scholar/ help.html**) are very good, so I won't take time to explain all of its functions. I would urge you, however, to make use of the advanced search feature, which has some useful limiters. You should also know that, under Scholar Preferences, you can set yourself up to be able to download citations from GS to a bibliographic manager like RefWorks or EndNote (more on bibliographic managers in chapter 7).

Here are some of the common types of citations you can expect to find in Google Scholar:

> ➤ Journal Articles—Look for the journal name just under the title link in the citation.

> ➤ Books—Not the full text in most cases; designated by [Book]

> ➤ Citations—This is a bit tricky—a citation is a reference to a scholarly article or book found within one of the articles or books in the GS database. So it's a reference to a reference. As such, it has no link to take you to a place where you can obtain it, though you can link to the source that referred to it, as well as do a search on Google to see if it's available on the open Net. This type of source is designated as [Citation].

> ➤ Conference Proceedings—These results have no special designation to tell them apart from journal articles, so you have to look at how they are described under the title link in the citation. Here's an example:

<u>From WEB to GRID, a new perspective for archaeology</u>
G Pelfer, PG Pelfer—Nuclear Science Symposium Conference Record, 2003
IEEE, 2003—ieeexplore.ieee.org
... In addition to the above—mentioned sites, **Iraq** houses some of the most
important archaeological collections of the world, such as the **Iraqi Museum**
of Baghdad....
<u>Cited by 2</u>—<u>Related Articles</u>—<u>Web Search</u>—<u>Import into RefWorks</u>

Note the name of the conference under the title. As long as we are looking
at this entry, note also that you can find out what sources referred to (cited)
this conference address, you can identify related (= similar) articles, and you
can import the citation into a bibliographic manager (if you set this up in
Scholar Preferences).

> ➢ Academic, government, etc. Web sites—These will be identifiable
> because they have URLs instead of journal names or descriptions like
> [Book] or [Citation].

6.3.3 CiteSeer (http://citeseer.ist.psu.edu/)

CiteSeer is a search engine for academic scientific information that is freely
available on the WWW. As such, it offers real full text. But it does a lot more.
In the scientific and social scientific worlds, the value of research papers is
often determined by how many other papers refer to (cite) them. If your paper
has had a hundred citations to it in other people's papers, it will be considered
to be more valuable to the scientific community than if it has had only one
citation. CiteSeer is able to break down the details of the articles it lists so that
you can see what sources each article cited and which articles have cited that
article. There are also a number of sort features to reorganize search results.

Citations to an existing paper can also help scholars follow a trail of
research on a topic: Paper A, published in 1998, is cited by paper B in 2000,
paper C in 2004, paper D in 2008, and so on. These later papers demonstrate
how the research in Paper A is being used in new ways to expand knowledge,
creating a history trail related to the development of the topic.

6.3.4 Scirius (http://www.scirus.com/srsapp/)

This site bills itself as "the most comprehensive science-specific search engine on
the Internet." The content provided includes both journal articles and academic

Web sites though some of the journal material is content from commercial databases like Elsevier's *Science Direct*. Thus, you may or may not have direct free access to electronic full text.

Scirius allows you to limit your search to journal articles, "preferred" Web sites or "other" Web sites, or any combination of these. You can sort results by relevance or date. Scirius also offers a clustering feature that gives you links to terminology you can use to narrow your search. Its advanced search offers quite a range of limiters to help you find the most focused results. You can also export your results so that they can be pulled into a bibliographic manager.

6.3.5 Windows Live Academic (http://academic.live.com)

A relative newcomer to academic search, Windows Live Academic (henceforth WLA) suffers from simply having too small a database, though the situation should improve over the coming years. WLA has a cool look to it and some interesting features:

> ➤ You can specify searches for particular authors or limit results to journals or conferences (but only after you have done your initial search; an advanced search feature is not available).

> ➤ You can sort by relevance or date (ascending or descending).

> ➤ You can move your mouse over a citation result to open up a full record on the right.

> ➤ You can do a direct download to one of several bibliographic managers.

Thus, while it is one of the more user-friendly WWW-based academic search engines, WLA needs much more content to make it successful. Maybe, by the time you read this, the content will be there.

6.3.6 getCITED (http://www.getcited.org/)

This is an interesting experiment in the interactivity of Web 2.0. Academic users of this search engine submit their own material or citations to it and have the ability (if properly signed in) to revise anything in the database. Think of it as the Wikipedia of academic search engines. In this case, why don't we let it speak for itself? The following is from the getCITED home page:

"**getCITED** is an online, member-controlled academic <u>database</u>, <u>directory</u> and <u>discussion</u> <u>forum</u>. Its contents are entered and edited by members of the academic community. By putting its content in the hands of its members, **getCITED** makes it possible to enter in and search for publications of *all* types. This means that, in addition to the books and articles accessible with other databases, book chapters, conference papers, working papers, reports, papers in conference proceedings, and other such research outlets can all be entered and then searched for within getCITED. In addition, getCITED makes it possible to link publications with all the publications in their bibliographies, thereby making possible a wide variety of publication and citation reports." (**http://www.getcited.org/**)

More of these types of free online academic search tools will emerge over time, fuelled in part by the growing open access movement that is making academic information available for free. But be warned—much of what you want is still only to be found within the journal databases your library pays for. The myth that most journal articles are freely available on the open Web is as believable as the alligators in New York City sewers.

6.4 Search Engines for the Rest of Humanity— Google and Friends

6.4.1 Searching by Search Engine, Using Keywords

In the most common Internet research situation, you want information on a topic, but you don't have a specific address. This is where a search engine can help you by taking the keyword(s) you input and searching the WWW for data that is relevant. As you will soon discover, each search engine does the job a bit differently and with different results.

Some search engines are better for certain searches than for others. Some *rank* the data they are giving you. That is, they assign probability percentages to tell you how likely it is that the search engine gave you what you asked for. Typically, you will get thousands of hits for any keyword search. Thus a search engines that has a good ranking procedure and doesn't give you more than you asked for is better for most searches.

How do you input the keywords? That depends. Each search engine has its own set of search paradigms. Most search engines have a "tips" or "help" or "about" link you can click on to be guided on the best ways to input keywords for that search engine.

> ➤ In most cases, search engines automatically create an AND. Commonly you can leave it out, but you have to specify OR. The NOT term is often done with a dash in front of a word (-trees). If you want to include in your search a word that is not normally searched (e.g., "the" or "of"), you will need to put a plus sign in front of the word, with no spaces: +the. Note that + signs are no longer used to create AND searches in most searches engines, as they once were.

> ➤ Most search engines allow you to group words that normally belong together. To do this, use quotation marks:

"accountability groups"

If you don't use the quotation marks, the search engine will also locate any articles that use the two words even though they are not related, as in:

"The president is calling for more *accountability*. This has been rejected by several *groups* of protestors who insist that ..."

Always check the search tips for a search engine and make sure you know what you're dealing with. Some search engines want you to input names in certain ways. Others want you to use capitals for proper names and titles. Most will allow you to refine your search if you find you're not getting what you want or you have too many hits.

6.4.2 A Basic Introduction to the Best Search Engines

Truth to tell (and I usually try to be truthful, because I'm not a convincing liar), you could likely get by with Google (www.google.com) and never use another search engine. But it can be useful to attempt a search on another search engine once you've googled, just in case you missed something. Each search engine creates its own index of the Internet, so that, while Google's is the biggest, it may not have included sites that are found in another search engine's index.

When I produced the second edition of this book, the best search engines were: Google, Vivisimo, Teoma, and AllTheWeb. Of these, Google and Vivisimo are still around, but Teoma is now essentially Ask.com (formerly Ask Jeeves) and AllTheWeb has been taken over by Yahoo.com (though it still exists on its own site as well). In the meantime, MSN has produced the Windows Live search engine, which resembles Google but has some unique features.

You need to be aware, though, that the search engines described below cover the World Wide Web as a whole. The quality of the individual sites in each index varies from the most scholarly to some guy who thinks he's a duck. You are the gatekeeper now, and evaluation is all important (more on this later in the chapter). Some professors simply won't accept Web sites in bibliographies unless you can prove that the material has been produced by a reputable scholars or at least people who have advanced knowledge of the topic.

By the time you read this, a new search engine may have arisen and the features of those described below may have changed. But I dare to introduce them to you anyway, brave fool that I am. Here goes:

Google (http://www.google.com/)

Google has the biggest index of the Net and consistently does the best job of locating what you're searching for. Here are some key features:

> As you input keywords to use as search tools, Google automatically forms them into an AND search and seeks to bring you Web sites that contain those words in close proximity to one another.

> Google uses a technique called PageRank that prioritizes your results by giving you first those sites that are most often found as links on other Web sites. This "popularity" measure really seems to work in most searches so that the most relevant sites appear in the first 20 or so results.

> Google offers simple techniques to create Boolean searches:

- AND is automatic

- You can create an OR by inputting OR. Google will nest searches with () as in **Freud (ego OR id)**, but if you are not sure it's working, use the advanced search (putting **Freud** into "with all of the words" and **ego id** into "with at least one of the words.")

- Phrases can be searched by putting quotation marks around them, e.g., **"apple trees."** This is true of all the best search engines. Or you can use Google's phrase search among advanced search features.

- You can't truncate search words, e.g., **educat*** for education, educator, etc. This feature simply doesn't work on Google.

➢ Have you ever discovered a site only to get a "Not found" message, possibly indicating that the site has been closed or has moved? If that happens in Google, you can click on the "Cached" link in the Google results list and get Google's snapshot of the Web site as it was when Google last indexed it.

➢ Google has links on its search page to allow you to toggle among various formats for its results—Web, Images, Video, News, Maps, and so on.

➢ Google offers a toolbar that you can download and install at the top of your browser. With it, you always have a Google box to do a search any time your browser is open. But there's more: The search terms you use appear on the toolbar so you can click on one of them and be taken to all the places in a document where that word appears. There is a separate search button on the toolbar that lets you do a search only within a Web site you currently have open. The toolbar can even limit the number of "popups" you experience (those annoying ads that pop up without you asking for them). Only the rare computer I ever use escapes without me adding a Google toolbar to it.

➢ Google has a pretty good "Advanced Search" feature that helps you do all sorts of things:

- The "Find Results" options let you build complex Boolean searches.

- You can specify the languages of the Web sites you want returned.

- You can ask for return of results only in specified formats (PDF, MS Word, PowerPoint, etc.), all of which are indexed in Google unlike some search engines.

- You can select only the most recently updated Web sites.

- You can specify where you want your search terms to appear in documents you retrieve.

- You can ask for only those sites belonging to a certain domain (registered Internet name).

- You can even locate the Web sites that have links to a specified site.

- You can specify searches within US Government and some University sites.

Google also offers separate search functions for books (Google Book—**http://books.google.com**), scholarly material (Google Scholar—**http://scholar.google.com**), blogs (Google Blog Search—**http://blogsearch.google.com**), things to buy (Google Product Search—**http://www.google.com/prdhp?tab=wf&ie=UTF-8**), and so on. All of these are found under the "more" link on the Google home page, or you can put icons to any of them into your Google toolbar.

All in all, Google is a winner.

Yahoo (http://search.yahoo.com/)

Yahoo has been a web portal longer than it has been a credible search engine. In fact, Yahoo's search function used Google until early 2004. Back in 2003 Yahoo acquired three search engines—AltaVista, AlltheWeb and Inktomi—then announced that it would no longer support any of them as they had been. Instead Yahoo built its own search engine out of the features of these older products (with great similarity to Inktomi). Since Yahoo is a popular site, its search engine is also popular. Here are some features:

As with Google, Yahoo offers links to allow searches to toggle among formats—web, images, video, etc. The result lists are very much like Google's, offering a "cached" link and a link for "more from this site." With the advanced search features you can build complex Boolean searches, specify more recently updated sites, choose your domain type (e.g., com, edu), a particular file format for results, level of filtering of objectionable material, and country/language of your results. An additional limiter is the ability to search only "Creative Commons" licensed material. Creative Commons is used by open access web publishing to enable people to post their material for free while at the same time protecting authors' rights.

A number of Web sites now offer the ability to do simultaneous Google and Yahoo searches with the results appearing side by side. See, for example **http://twingine.com/** and **http://www.googleguy.de/google-yahoo/**. If these sites have disappeared by the time you read this, simply do a search in Google with the terminology: **Google Yahoo.**

Is Yahoo as good as Google? My bias would still be in favor of Google, because it has a longer track record, usually finds me what I need, and has better options for advanced searching. But using more than one search engine is a smart idea. Each has its own index of Web sites, so results will be different. As a second choice, Yahoo is a good option.

Windows Live (http://www.live.com/)

Windows Live is the successor to MSN search and now is used as MSN's search engine as well as functioning on its own in a clean Google-like site. Many search engines are taking on a dreadful sameness, displaying results similarly, offering similar advanced search features, and so on. At this point, Windows Live is not working with as large a number of Web sites as Google and Yahoo, but it does have a few features to relieve the boredom of simply imitating Google.

First, it provided, before Google did, links to images, news and so on, which you can just click on without retyping your original web page search. Thus a **Badke William** search for all things me can be turned into an image search with one click (Google now has this too).

Second, it has an advanced search that allows you to add Boolean terms in various combinations, but you will only see the advanced search on your results page. You can also customize your home page, adding weather, news, stocks, etc. (all the things that potentially annoy the researcher who just wants to do a search).

Ask.com (http://www.ask.com/)

To round out our account of the best search engines, we have Ask.com, formerly Ask Jeeves and built on the Teoma search engine. True, Ask has cooler icons and a number of nice skins available, but its look on the surface is just like Google. Its advanced search features are quite Google-like though more limited than Google's.

But hark. Is there something new on the horizon? A glance at the results page shows that for many searches there has been a real attempt to bring something fresh to the table. On the left are some clustering features—links that enable you to narrow your search to some aspect of whatever you were looking for. On the right are Images, Video and News links, the first two with picture icons. Rather than toggling among various formats, you can do your search and see the other formats also displayed. Thus if I search on Toyota Camry, I get on the left links to narrower features like Toyota Camry Repair and Toyota Camry Accessories. On the right I get thumbnails of pictures and video along with links to news stories.

For clustering search engines, see Chapter 3.3.2 above.

6.4.3 The New Semantic Search Engines

In 2008, Xerox released **FactSpotter** (URL not available at time of publication, so you'll need to Google: **FactSpotter**). Xerox bills it as a search engine that digs deeper and identifies what the searcher is looking for by analyzing the semantics of the search. Essentially, the software considers words in their context (other words in the search) to determine what word meaning is wanted. For example, a search on **Lincoln Vice President** will connect the name Lincoln with Abraham Lincoln because of the reference to Vice President, and will bring back information on his first vice president, Hannibal Hamlin. (Interestingly, Google, without semantic analysis, brought up the same information).

Many other semantic search engines are under development. These tools are pointing the way forward to new ways of searching. For more on the concept of the semantic search engine, see **http://www.webmasterworld.com/forum5/4474.htm**

6.5 Searching by Subject Tree

All information exists within hierarchies. For example, cell phones are a subclass of telephones which are a subclass of electronic communication devices, which are a subclass of all communication devices.

Information hierarchies form a tree like structure. There are certain sites on the Internet where you can search down various hierarchies or subject trees from more general categories to specific ones.

For example, Google, while majoring on keyword searches, also has a Directory (**http://www.google.com/dirhp**) that leads you to a list of categories like Art, Business, News, Science, and so on. Click on any one, and you can follow a hierarchy down to more specific information.

6.6 Portals

A growing area of significant development on the Internet is the "portal," a site that serves as an introduction to important Internet sites on a subject. Typically, its main feature is a collection of links to sites that have been checked out for quality. What you end up with is a hierarchical way of searching the Net without a search engine. Its advantage is that someone has evaluated the sites, so you have a better chance of finding material that you can actually use (though your own critical thinking skills still need to be engaged—Sorry, I'm sure you immediately assumed that using a portal meant you wouldn't have to do much thinking).

Portals are organized by subject. Here are a few examples:

> Psych Web (**http://www.psywww.com/**) is a psychology portal to Web sites categorized by type. Locate a category like Scholarly Issues, and it will lead you to a page that subcategorizes web links under headings like Cross-Cultural Psychology, Hypnosis, etc.

> History on the Web (**http://www.lib.washington.edu/subject/History/tm/**)

> Biology Online—Information in the Life Sciences (**http://biology-online.org/**)

> Wabash Center Internet Guide to Religion (**http://www.wabashcenter.wabash.edu/resources/guide_headings.aspx**)

But how do you locate such sites in the first place? Here's where a more general portal can help. A general portal is usually much larger, and often serves, at least in part, as a doorway to more specific subject portals. For example:

> Infomine: Scholarly Internet Academic Collections (**http://infomine.ucr.edu/**) boasts over 100,000 academically valuable sites, organized by broad subject categories or searchable by its internal search engine. Many of the sites it lists are actually subject portals.

> Multimedia Educational Resource for Learning and Online Teaching (**http://www.merlot.org/**). This is a project of several universities and academic organizations to organize and peer review Web sites valuable for higher education. You can search it directly or hierarchically by subject categories.

> Academic Info (**http://www.academicinfo.net/**) is an educational subject directory to programs of study and test preparation sites. It includes a section of subject gateways to most disciplines.

> Librarians' Index to the Internet (**http://lii.org/**) is searchable directly or through hierarchies.

6.7 The Hidden Internet

You may have heard of the so-called "Hidden Internet" or "Invisible Web" or "Deep Web." It's billed as that portion of the Net that only the chosen few can see. Before you start thinking in terms of nasty conspiracies, recognize that there may be legitimate reasons for certain Web information not to be easily found.

6.7.1 What do we mean by "Hidden?"

A simple definition of "hidden" in this context would be: "Any information carried on the Internet that can't easily be found by a search engine." Considering the fact that all search engines must first "discover" information before they can index it, there is always a strong possibility that some sites will remain hidden. Beyond these are sites that search engines did find but that have deeper portions accessible only through a password.

6.7.2 What's the nature of the Hidden Internet?

The Hidden Internet includes the following:

➢ Sites that are password protected—corporate intranets, subscription databases, banking information, e-mail accounts, and so on. These are protected either to maintain security or restrict access only to patrons who are entitled to be there.

➢ Information within non-restricted databases such as library catalogs. A search engine may find a library catalog or other database, but it won't get past the front door to identify/view individual records within that database. Why? Because the Internet search engine can't actually search the database, which has its own search engine. So you might find the catalog of a university library with Google, but Google can't search that catalog automatically to find a record for a certain book. You have to search it yourself.

➢ New or obscure sites not yet indexed by a search engine, or not indexed by the search engine you are using.

6.7.3 How do I find information on the Hidden Internet?

That depends. If it is a password-protected site, you need to be authorized or you'll need to pay to get access. Don't hack!

Many searchable databases can be located either by search engine or by hierarchical searches on the Net (see the above section). Gary Price has put up a site called *direct search* (**http://www.freepint.com/gary/direct.htm**) to guide you to sites that open doors to the Hidden Internet.

The Hidden Internet lives, but there's no conspiracy. Really!

6.8 Evaluating Information from the Internet

Let's be realistic for a moment (aren't we always?) and ask the question: *Why would people with data want to put it up for free on the Internet?* The answers are varied:

- ➢ They want to sell you something, and their web page is simply advertising or a doorway to a credit card purchase.

- ➢ They have something they want to say, and this a cheap and easy way to do it. Here you can have anything from *"Hi, I'm Tim, and here are some pictures of my iguana Frank,"* to *"I was abducted by Martians, and I want to warn the world before they destroy us all."* Here too are the blogs and social networking sites like MySpace and Facebook.

- ➢ A government or public agency that would normally not charge for its information wants to make it available. Here you can find everything from the ERIC Database to census data, and so on.

- ➢ An educational body sees providing information as part of its mandate. Here you may get open access journal articles, electronic editions of out-of-print books, guides to this and that, occasionally even electronic dictionaries or encyclopedias.

- ➢ Sincere scholars and other individuals who have valuable information to share and want to make that information freely available for the edification of everyone.

But take careful note of one foundational rule of life: **Few people, except those related to all but the first reason above, provide information for free on** the Net unless they can't find anyone to pay for it or they have the financial resources to give it away freely.

What does that mean for you, the anxious Internet searcher? It means several things:

> A lot of what you hoped might be on the Net is not there or you have to pay for it—the full texts of most journal articles, the full texts of recent books, a vast array of reference tools, etc.

> Most keyword searches through search engines also bring you a ton of less than wonderful Web sites that you have to weed through to find a few gems.

> It's difficult to evaluate the quality of the material you find on the Net. Let's consider this latter point a bit more closely. In normal publishing, there are gatekeepers to make sure that material that is inferior doesn't get published (at least we hope there are gatekeepers). On the Internet, anybody who wants to say anything has the chance to say it. Unless it is criminally obscene, violently racist or a clear and present danger to society, no one challenges it. Thus people can tell lies on the Net, and they probably won't suffer any nasty consequences (at least not in this life).

So what happens when you download a document that has no author clearly named but seems to be reliable information about B.F. Skinner's behaviorism? How do you determine whether it's good or bad information? Here are some clues:

> Look for the name of an author and/or organization responsible for the information. One way to do this is to recognize that Internet URLs are hierarchical and that the slashes in an address (/) define levels of the hierarchy. For example, the Web site advertising my book, *Beyond the Answer Sheet: Academic Success for International Students* (an example showing my penchant for blatant self promotion) has the URL **http://www.acts.twu.ca/lbr/answer_sheet.htm**. If I chop off the portion/**lbr/answer_sheet.htm**, I have the root left: **http://www.acts. twu.ca**, which is the educational institution that has allowed me access to their Web site because I am one of them. Chopping back on a URL will often lead you to the source behind the document you're interested in, though sometimes it just reveals the name of a person's Internet service provider, which, if it's some generic vendor of web space, will give you no help at all.

➤ Look for signs of scholarship—good language level, analytical thinking, bibliography and/or footnotes, logical organization.

➤ Look for signs of a *lack* of scholarship—lots of opinion without the support of evidence, indications of paranoia (as in *somebody's out to get us,* or *we're victims of a conspiracy*), poor spelling and grammar, lack of references to other sources, poor organization.

➤ Ask yourself—does this person have a vested interest in promoting a viewpoint or is he/she simply sharing information? Vested interests may be OK as long as you are well aware of what they are. A site selling Toyotas is going to be different in its very nature from a site offering independent reviews of Toyotas.

Ultimately, you will have to evaluate the information itself. Does it make sense? Does it ring true? Is there sufficient backing for viewpoints presented? Have you or your professor ever heard of the people involved? Remember that Internet data may lack all the proper signposts of good scholarly work and yet still be valuable. On the other hand, it may have footnotes and a bibliography but be a racist rant. For proper evaluation, the buck stops with you actually reading the material and making sense of it.

If you want some help learning how to evaluate Internet resources, take The Internet Detective, a free Web site tutorial with quizzes. It's very cool. (**http://www.vts.intute.ac.uk/detective/**).

6.9 Some Internet Addresses Valuable for Research Purposes

In presenting the following addresses, I must warn you again that addresses, like phone numbers, go out of date fairly quickly. On the Net, something you found today might not be there tomorrow. So, some of these addresses may not work. If you have a problem, try searching for the title of the source, using a search engine.

6.9.1 Reference Sources

The Internet Public Library: **http://www.ipl.org/**
Refdesk, an amazingly detailed site that bills itself as "The single best source for facts" (**http://www.refdesk.com/**)

A biography encyclopedia: **http://www.biography.com/**

6.9.2 Searchable Library Catalogs

Libdex: **http://www.libdex.com/**. (For this one, it's best to click on the "Country" link).
Library of Congress searchable catalog: **http://catalog.loc.gov/**
WorldCat: **http://www.worldcat.org/**

6.9.3 Directories

Switchboard (addresses & phone numbers—US plus Yellow Pages): **http://www.switchboard.com/**
Canada 411 (Canadian phone numbers & addresses): **http://www.canada411.ca/**

6.10 For Further Study

Study Guide

1. What exactly is the Internet? How does it relate to the World Wide Web?
2. Define the following terms: browser, home page, URL, search engine, World Wide Web, document, link, bookmark.
3. Why are free journals to a large degree an academic myth?
4. What's the difference between a scholarly search engine and ordinary search engines? What are the names of some scholarly search engines and what do they provide?
5. What are the top search engines on the Net?
6. What are "subject trees" on the Internet, and how can they help you?
7. What are Internet portals, and how can they help you?
8. What is the hidden Internet? How do you find information within it?
9. What are the key means by which you can evaluate the quality of information on Internet sites? Why is more evaluation required for Internet sites than for regularly published books and articles?

Practice with the Internet

1. Try an identical search on several search engines (e.g., Google, Yahoo, Windows Live, Ask.com). Why do some search engines come up with results different from others? Is it a correct assumption that **google.com** will most often produce better results than other search engines? [If you can't think of topics to search try the following: Skinner and behaviorism and Walden; Lucrezia Borgia (or is it Lucretia Borgia?); Bill Gates and antitrust.]

2. Take the Internet Detective tutorial: (**http://www.vts.intute.ac.uk/detective/**)

Assignment

Answer the following questions, using one of these search engines: **google.com, search.yahoo.com, live.com** or **ask.com**. In each case indicate the keywords you searched with and URL(s) of the site(s) that had the answer:

a. It is believed that a European theologian, possibly Emil Brunner or Karl Barth, said that everything important he'd ever learned about theology came from the song "Jesus loves me this I know, for the Bible tells me so." If you can verify that the statement was actually made, indicate what its wording was, who said it, and (if possible) under what circumstances it was originally spoken or written down. Note that some of the sites you find will not be particularly academic and may simply be parroting a rumor that is not accurate. Try to find a site that gives an authoritative answer.

b. The following is a real question asked by an academic library user. Find the correct citation, including author, title, journal, volume number, date, and page numbers:

    A professor here needs help clarifying a citation. He already has a photocopy of the article, but needs to know the volume, issue, and date in which the piece was published. The information we have is:
    Author: Joachim Begrich
    Title: Das priesterliche Heilsorakel
    Journal: Zeitschrift fur die altestamentliche Wissenschaft (ZAW)

c. In 1948, the Behaviourist psychologist B.F. Skinner wrote a novel entitled *Walden Two.* Find an Internet site for fans of the book and locate within that site an article about the book. What's the URL for the site and what's the title of the article?

d. The following quotation is plagiarized from a source on the Internet. Identify the URL of the original source:

"Jack the Ripper! Few names in history are as instantly recognizable. Fewer still evoke such vivid images: noisome courts and alleys, hansom cabs and gaslights, swirling fog, prostitutes decked out in the tawdriest of finery, the shrill cry of newsboys—and silent, cruel death personified in the capeshrouded figure of a faceless prowler of the night, armed with a long knife and carrying a black Gladstone bag."

7

Other Resources and Case Studies in Research

Sometimes you get desperate. All the normal research avenues narrow down to footpaths and then disappear entirely. You're running out of time and you have nothing to show for the hours you've spent. Now there's a need for innovative action. This chapter will try to steer you in new and potentially fascinating directions. Then, this being the most loosely organized chapter in the book, we'll also look at some other helpful resources, and then try out a couple of case studies of actual research projects.

7.1 Seeing Where We've Been

Before we launch you into new sources for research data, it's probably a good idea to rehearse where we've been. Maybe you've missed some important resources. Let's make a strategies list so that you can go back over your research methods to this point and check out possibilities that may have eluded you the first time you went through.

The Strategies We've Covered (Now for the First Time in One Place):

> ➤ *Get a working knowledge of your topic* (You went to reference sources, including the Internet, and became familiar with the basics.) Ask yourself: Did your reference sources suggest other related topics or give a bibliography that you've overlooked? Are there other sources of reference information to look at? (see below)

➤ *Assess the research topic, narrow it, come up with an analytical research question and suggest a preliminary outline:* Did you set the topic so narrowly that there are insufficient resources? Or did you fail to set it narrowly enough and now you have a fuzzy view of what your topic is? Often the problem with finding relevant sources is that you are not focusing clearly on what the research project is setting out to do. You need to be able to express your research question or thesis in *one sentence* that deals with *one issue or problem you want to try to solve.* More on this in Appendix One.

➤ *Do a search in a library catalog, using keywords and controlled vocabularies as needed:* Did you find everything that was there? If you began with a keyword search, you need to look closely at the catalog records you brought up. What controlled vocabulary subject headings were attached to the books you found? If you started with subject headings, did you find all the relevant ones? Looking at the records you've brought up may help you to discover other possible subject headings or narrower approaches to the topic. Did you consider books that might *contain* information relevant to you? E.g., for a paper on abortion, perhaps some key works in medical ethics might have relevant chapters on abortion.

➤ *Do a search for journal articles:* Did you use the right journal databases for the topic? Did you investigate the searching requirements for those databases? Did you choose narrow enough keywords or controlled vocabulary terms? Are you sure you checked your library's journal holdings carefully?

➤ *Make a judicious search of Internet resources.* Here, use your best evaluative skills and be sure you know what your professor will allow you to include in your research project.

Now let's consider some options you may not have thought of:

7.2 Full Text Reference Tools

There is a growing number of reference works that are available in electronic format or which have a CD that accompanies the print version. Each library will have its own collection of such tools, often available through your library home page or catalog. These resources are different from Google search results or Wikipedia (see Chapter Two) in that they have come through the more traditional publishing process of editors and expert writers (gatekeeping). Your professors will thus see them as reliable, even in electronic form.

On the World Wide Web, the availability of reference sources that use traditional production and editing procedures is pretty limited. Here's a wildly eclectic list of examples chosen at a whim for reasons I no longer recall:

➢ *Academic Guide to Jewish History*: **http://www.library.utoronto.ca/ jewishhistory/**

➢ *Cambridge History of English and American Literature* (1907–1921, searchable by keyword and thesaurus): **http://www.bartleby.com/ cambridge/**

➢ *The Canadian Encyclopedia*: **http://www.thecanadianencyclopedia.com**

➢ *Encyclopedia Smithsonian*: **http://www.si.edu/Encyclopedia_SI/**

➢ *Stanford Encyclopedia of Philosophy*: **http://plato.stanford.edu/**

➢ *TechEncyclopedia* (definitions of terms in technology and computing): **http://www.techweb.com/encyclopedia/**

➢ WolframMathWorld (a mathematics encyclopedia): **http://mathworld. wolfram.com/**

7.3 ERIC

One of the great untapped resources for research is ERIC. No, this is not a linebacker on a sophomore football team. ERIC stands for Education Resources Information Center, a clearinghouse that makes available studies, reports, curriculum helps, etc. produced by educational institutions.

But don't think of it just as an educational database. Educators are concerned about virtually anything that might be related to education, from the effects of early poverty on adult job performance, to the ramifications of teen suicide. This means that a wide range of topics in the social sciences are covered, as well as quite a few areas of the humanities.

Rather than have schools, colleges and universities put their studies on the issues affecting their work into filing cabinets, never to be seen again, the U.S. government arranged to collect these studies and make them available to libraries. To do this, ERIC needed to have a two part approach:

> ➤ The reports themselves. They could be anything from a study of the effects of TV violence on high schoolers in Salem, Oregon, to an analysis of dyslexia in relation to reading speed in Podunk Junction. Such reports could be under 50 pages in length, though they might sometimes go to 100 pages or more. Older ERIC documents (i.e., these gathered reports) are primarily available on microfiche. Now close to two decades of more recent ERIC documents are freely available in PDF full text and more of the older material is being digitized.

> ➤ A database with which to search the ERIC documents for topics of interest. Here the government had a stroke of genius—why not put the database on the Internet so that anyone could search it from anywhere? What is more, all ERIC documents for which electronic full text was available could be linked to the citations in the databases and downloaded by users for free.

One further bit of information which sometimes confuses users—as ERIC grew, the database added a journals component to enable people to identify journal articles in education. The confusing part is that *ERIC itself does not provide the electronic full text of these journal articles. You will need to locate them yourself.* Thus you actually have two databases in one. To distinguish ERIC Documents from ERIC journals, the former were designated ED—so that each ERIC Document has a code number that looks like this: ED213562. ERIC Journals are designated EJ, as in: EJ498231. You can find both EJs and EDs in a single search, though it's possible to specify a search for only journals or only documents.

In 2003, the U.S. government announced that it was consolidating the various subject clearinghouses that collected ERIC documents and was going to put ERIC under the control of a single contractor who would be charged with creating a new Internet interface and moving ERIC much more into an electronic full text environment. This has actually turned out quite well, with more full text ERIC documents now available and more recent documents being added.

While you may also be able to access it through journal database vendors like EBSCO, ERIC amazingly is available freely on the Internet and includes the full text content at no charge as well.

Here are some of the key searching features:

> ➤ You can do a basic search, specifying what field (portion of the record for a document) you want to search, e.g., author, title, subject heading, keywords.

- ➤ There is an advanced search that will allow searching more than one field at once, along with the use of Boolean operators.

- ➤ There is a thesaurus, so that you can browse for subject headings. ERIC, in fact, has a very sophisticated thesaurus and detailed records for each document it indexes.

- ➤ There is a "Search help" link, if you get confused.

Don't ignore ERIC. It is a very good resource for many kinds of research. The fact that you can access its database and much of its full text on the Internet makes it all the more helpful.

7.4 Government Documents

Various governments produce vast hosts of information which can be found in libraries, can be purchased, or can be discovered free on the Internet (depending on what the information is). Publications put out by governments cover potentially every area of life. The only problem is that they are notoriously difficult to find. If you are in a library that has government documents, rely on your reference librarian to guide you through the maze.

For US government information on the World Wide Web, you can go to **http://www.access.gpo.gov/su_docs/fdlp/ec**. This site can help you find materials by agency or by topic. It even offers you guidance to locate documents in libraries. (In case the address goes out of date, the site name is "FDLP Electronic Collection." Google that phrase, and the site should come up.) For state government information, try the portal produced by the Library of Congress: **http://www.loc.gov/rr/news/stategov/stategov.html**.

If you are blessed enough to live in Canada, as I do, the Internet site you want is: **http://www.canada.gc.ca/main_e.html**.

For other country governments, try: **http://www.ipl.org/div/subject/browse/law20.40.00/**

Not everything you need in government information, however, is on the Net. As with every other source of information, some is online and some is only accessible in print. Certain libraries are designated as depository collections that receive print forms of government information. To locate the depository library near you in the US, go to **http://www.gpoaccess.gov/libraries.html**, and in Canada to **http://dsp-psd.pwgsc.gc.ca/Depo/table-e.html**. For other countries, Google the following: **depository libraries countryname**.

7.5 Doctoral Dissertations

It sounds so intriguing, so right—if you want the best cutting edge research on a topic, why not locate a few doctoral dissertations? But the realities can be a mixed bag.

The searching tool for dissertations is *ProQuest Dissertations & Theses Database,* an electronic tool available in larger libraries but very few small ones. It's fully searchable and you can easily locate citations and abstracts (summaries) of doctoral work on your topic. ProQuest offers with its databases the full text of close to a million dissertations, for those libraries that can afford to provide this feature. For libraries that can't, or for older dissertations not available in full text, you may be able to use interlibrary loan (not always successful) or buy the dissertation yourself from ProQuest. There is a PDF tutorial at **http://training.proquest.com/trc/training/en/pqdd.pdf.**

A suggestion: Before you go on a long quest for a dissertation, search for the author's name in your catalog and/or a larger catalog like WorldCat (**http://www.worldcat.org/**). It's possible that the dissertation was later published as an academic book, making interlibrary loan unnecessary. You might even convince your local librarian to buy the book.

7.6 Bibliographic Managers

For some time now there have been computer programs available to help you save citations to books, articles, Web sites, and so on. These Bibliographic Managers enable you to collect citations in specified folders and generate bibliographies in most any format you want. What is more, the most popular of them—RefWorks and EndNote—are not only now web-based, but offer the option of adding a plug-in to your word processing program so that you can create automatic citations and bibliographies without having to type in the information yourself. Let's take a quick look at each of them:

7.6.1 EndNote

EndNote allows you to download or import citations from various databases, search databases from within EndNote (though the search interface is not as sophisticated as searching a database directly), store citations in designated folders and even attach PDFs of the documents themselves. Since it is all

Internet-based, it doesn't take up room on your hard drive (leaving you space for a few more music videos). You can configure Google Scholar (under "Scholar preferences") to create an import link to EndNote.

What is more, you can download Word templates to enable you to format a research paper properly. Even better, you can download a plug-in that enables you to zap citations right into your research paper and format them as well as create a bibliography in the bibliographic format of your choice.

7.6.2 RefWorks

RefWorks offers most of the features of EndNote except (as of 2007) the Word templates. It also has a plug-in for Internet Explorer to download WWW citations. Like EndNote, you can configure Google Scholar Preferences to import citations, and it has a word processing plug-in to insert citations and format them as well as create a bibliography.

7.6.3 Zotero (http://www.zotero.org/)

If your institution doesn't have access to RefWorks or EndNote, and you want to use a bibliographic manager, do not fear. Zotero is free and offers most of the strong features provided by commercial managers. It operates best with the Firefox browser. There's a free download for Firefox at **http://www.mozilla. com/en-US/firefox/**.

Happy researching with tools like these. They can be a great help.

7.7 Consulting with Friends, Mentors and Librarians

We live in a highly consultative age, and the tendency to run our ideas past other people is pretty strong. There are real and obvious reasons why trying out aspects of your project on others can bring fresh perspectives and help you make early or mid-course correctives. Being more of a solitary researcher myself, I may be too anti-social to write about collaboration, but here goes anyway.

7.7.1 What are Friends Good For?

Meetings of minds are usually helpful, at least in theory. Running ideas past your friends is generally a good idea. Be open to their suggestions. At the same time, recognize that you may already know more about the subject matter than your friends do. Thus taking advice from a friend because he/she seems smarter than you, or more experienced, or whatever, may not be the best choice. Trust your instincts and filter advice from friends carefully.

7.7.2 Consulting Professors

Your professors form a breed to themselves—intelligent, articulate, but they usually have far too much to do (which, I think, leads to the mythology of the absent-minded professor). If you are going to consult with a professor, have a clear question in mind and focus on being brief and to the point. For example, you might have something like this: "You listed a research topic as 'Charlemagne,' and I was wondering what you'd think of me approaching it this way ..." Professors should be consulted if you are unsure of what to do or what is being demanded, if you have thought of an approach to an assignment which may not be exactly what the professor is asking for, or if you are stuck somewhere in the research process and need advice to help you get unstuck.

7.7.3 Encountering Librarians

Research shows that many students have a very limited perspective on what librarians can do for them. Some believe librarians are good only for book and paper issues, because they know almost nothing about technology. Not so. Others see librarians as "generalists" who know a little bit about everything but, unlike professors, don't know a lot about any specific topic. Not so again. Actually, most librarians know more about information technology than either you or your professors do. If you need to use almost any database, a librarian is likely to offer more help than anyone else can. And if you are working on a highly specialized topic, a librarian has the skills to work with that topic and actually help you advance beyond where you are. Librarians are amazing people. Consult them frequently. They don't usually bite.

7.8 Case Studies in Research

It's all very well to read about the theory of research, but hands-on experience teaches us that we live in a complex world. Methods that may have worked perfectly well in one research project are disastrous in another. Keen minds and brave hearts are needed if we want to succeed in actually carrying out a research project. The moment you've been waiting for all along is here. Let's do some research!

7.8.1 "Teenage Suicide"

While the rates for teenage suicide dropped in the 1990s and early 2000s, they are growing again. For a sociology class, you've been given the above topic, and now you're dismayed at the possibilities. Should you prepare:

- ➤ A statistical analysis of the prevalence of the problem?
- ➤ A study of why the rate is growing?
- ➤ An analysis of the social situations of those who commit suicide?
- ➤ A study of suicide prevention methods?
- ➤ Any one of a dozen other possibilities?

Before you go too much farther, it's best to get a working knowledge. Let's consider a few reference tools, then move on to consider our approach:

Reference Sources.

After poking around the reference collection for awhile, I came across the *Gale Encyclopedia of Childhood and Adolescence*. While I thought this was a promising source, it has little on the suicide issue. So I turned to William Damon, ed. *Handbook of Child Psychology.* In volume 3 there is an interesting summary of the work of a researcher named Michael Chandler who shows evidence that suicide can result from teenagers losing "persistent identity over time." He observes that "Even temporarily losing the narrative thread of one's personal persistence ... leaves adolescents especially vulnerable to a range of self destructive impulses against which others remain better insulated." In balance to this view, I sought out a few more reference articles and built my knowledge both of the prevalence and characteristics of the problem.

Topic Analysis.

Chandler's premise is intriguing. Could it be that teenage suicide is rising in prevalence because people's lives are becoming more disrupted through job displacement, family breakup, youth violence, fears for the future and so on? If so, and if Chandler is right, the relatively fragile self-identities of teenagers may be more threatened today than they once were. Every disruption is an attack upon personal identity, leading to self-destructive thinking.

But how can I formulate this into a proper research question? I can do so by trying to capture the essence of what I want to find out. How about something like this: *If Chandler is correct that adolescent suicide is linked to loss of persistent identity over time, can the increasingly disruptive nature of modern life be seen as a factor in the growth of suicides among teenagers?*

A preliminary outline might look like this:
Introduction—the problem of a growing rate of teenage suicide
I. Chandler's persistent identity model in relation to other possible models.
II. Analysis of increased life disruption among modern adolescents in light of the growing suicide rate.
III. Comparison of modern life disruption with the elements described in Chandler's model.
Conclusion: The value of Chandler's model in explaining the increase in teen suicides.

Book Search

For a book search you have some options:

> You could do a controlled vocabulary *Library of Congress Subject Heading* search under the heading: **Teenagers—Suicidal behavior.** That will get you a list of titles like: *Adolescent Suicide, The Cruelest Death,* and *Students at Risk.* When you get down to reading them, you will have to look for references to Chandler's work or to themes similar to those of Chandler.

> You could do a controlled vocabulary subject search, using Chandler's name as a *subject heading* to find any books written about him and/or his views.

> You could get boldly adventurous and try a Boolean keyword search such as **Chandler AND suicide.** Here, you need to be careful. What kinds of keywords are being searched? Just title words? Titles and

authors? All the words in a catalog record? Depending on what key-words are being searched, you will find different resources. I tried this as a title keyword search and found nothing. Using a keyword search that covered the whole catalog record, I discovered two essays by Michael Chandler directly on the personal continuity issue. The search terms I used were found in the catalog record's contents descriptions for two books which were collections of essays: *Disorders and Dysfunctions of the Self,* and *Children, Youth and Suicide.* Without a Boolean keyword search, I probably would have missed these valu-able sources.

➢ You could do an author search for books by Michael Chandler. Trying this out, I found the following: Chandler, M. J., Lalonde, C. E., Sokol, B. W., & Hallett, D. (2003). *Personal persistence, identity, and suicide: A study of Native and non-Native North American adolescents.* Bingo!

Journal Database Search.

In searching for journal articles, the first question might be: "What subject dis-cipline are we dealing with?" It could be sociology or psychology or social psy-chology (life seldom fits neat categories, which is why librarians go a bit batty sometimes). Let's try PsycINFO.

The first search should try to identify articles by Chandler on the topic (these are, therefore, primary sources, i.e., straight from the horse's mount, not that I'm calling Chandler a horse). Going with the "Authors" option for the EBSCO interface of PsycINFO, you find his name and click on the check box.

Your search reveals, among other results, two essays from edited books and one journal article:

Chandler, M., & Lalonde, C. (1995). The problem of self-continuity in the con-text of rapid personal and cultural change. *The self in European and North American culture: Development and processes* (pp. 45-63). New York, NY, US: Kluwer Academic/Plenum Publishers.

Chandler, M. J., & Lalonde, C. (1998). Cultural continuity as a hedge against suicide in Canada's first nations. *Transcultural Psychiatry, 35*(2), 191-219.

Chandler, M., Lalonde, C., & Sokol, B. (2000). Continuities of selfhood in the face of radical developmental and cultural change. *Culture, thought, and development* (pp. 65-84). Mahwah, NJ, US: Lawrence Erlbaum Associates Publishers.

Now, if you want to find articles about Chandler and his views on identity, try something simple—a keyword search on **chandler and identity**. Beyond the usual articles by Chandler, you find two that are about his work:

Krettenauer, T. (2005). The role of epistemic cognition in adolescent identity formation: Further evidence. *Journal of Youth and Adolescence, 34*(3), 185-198.

Marcia, J. E. (2003). Treading fearlessly: A commentary on personal persistence, identity development, and suicide. *Monographs of the Society for Research in Child Development, 68*(2), 131-138.

A good start, but you had hoped for more about his work. How about searching him as a subject heading? Opening the record for the article by Marcia above, you find that this database has no entry for Chandler as a subject heading. But all is not lost. You can take any of the following subjects: **Suicide, Persistence, Self-identity**, and link it in an AND search with the keyword **Chandler**.

ERIC

ERIC should be the kind of database ideally suited to a topic like this one. Let's go ask ERIC. A search of **Chandler and suicide** finds us only three relevant citations, all of them journal articles already identified from PsycINFO. Let's try **adolescen* and suicide and identity**.

Two citations look useful, one an ERIC document (ED) and one a journal article (EJ):

DiPilato, Marina (1993) *Integration of Cultural Values in the Treatment of a Suicidal Adolescent.* Annual Meeting of the American Psychological Association (101st, Toronto, Ontario, Canada, August 20-24, 1993). (ERIC Document Reproduction Service No. ED370025.

Bar-Joseph, Hanna; Tzuriel, David (1990) Suicidal Tendencies and Ego Identity in Adolescence. *Adolescence Journal* 25(97), 215-223. [ERIC #:EJ412940]

Summary

Where are you now? You've identified books and articles related to rates of adolescent suicide and particularly to Michael Chandler's work. Probably the only thing remaining would be to dig into the sources you've found to discover who else agrees with Chandler and to find out whether or not there are dissenting opinions. Clearly there is more than enough research information out there to provide you with the resources you need. Your goal, remember, is to discover whether or not Chandler's theory is an adequate explanation of the growth in teen suicides.

Let's try one more topic, this time in the area of history:

7.8.2 "Lucrezia Borgia"

For a course on Renaissance History, you've been asked to write a research paper on a significant figure of the Renaissance period. For some strange reason, you think of the sinister femme fatale of the early 1500's, Lucrezia Borgia.

Reference Sources.

For a topic like this, any number of reference sources would do, even general encyclopedias like *Americana* or *Britannica*. There are also specific dictionaries and encyclopedias related to the history of Lucrezia's era. The *Britannica* entry provides good background and points out that Lucrezia (1480–1519) had a bad reputation for criminal activity, though it is possible that other family members were the real perpetrators (interesting!). She was a patron of the arts, etc. The *New Catholic Encyclopedia* has a good article on the **Borgia family**, something you will probably also have to study.

Topical Analysis.

While you could simply write a short biography of Lucrezia Borgia, true research demands more. The controversy over her supposed criminal and treacherous behavior would make a far better project.

Why not focus on this research question: *Who was the real Lucrezia Borgia?* A preliminary outline might look like this:

Introduction (to Lucrezia and her times)
I. Her reputation for treachery.
II. Possible evidence for her innocence.
Conclusion

Note that you will still have to relate Lucrezia's history, but now you are doing it around a definite focus.

Book search.

Because you are dealing with a person, the task of determining subject headings and keywords is significantly easier than it was with your last case study. Presumably, you can do a Library of Congress Subject Heading search under her name: **Borgia, Lucrezia**, though you may want as well to search for material on her relatives or even on the heading **Borgia Family**. If you find that these materials are limited in number, you might need to find books on Italian Renaissance history that will contain material on the Borgias.

You could also try a bibliography search using sources you have already located. One problem that may arise is that Lucrezia was Italian. Thus, many bibliography sources may be in a language you don't understand.

Journal Databases.

Once again, the main challenge is choosing the right database to search. Why not try a broad based tool like EBSCO Academic Search Premier (though your institution may have a different broad-based database like ProQuest or InfoTrac or FirstSearch)? No matter what database you use, you are going to discover that the results are limited and often mixed with book reviews and references to the opera based on her life. There just does not appear to be a great deal of journal literature on her. (A quick search on Google Scholar confirms this). Still, reviews can lead you to key books on the subject and can provide a critique of those books.

Attempting to be brilliant, you decide at this point to do a lateral and try a Google search on **"Lucrezia Borgia" bibliography**. This leads you to an About.com site with links to several articles about Lucrezia and to several bibliographies you can use to identify other resources (**http://europeanhistory. about.com/od/borgialucrezia/Borgia_Lucrezia.htm**—watch out for some really annoying popups on this site).

In the examples above, you probably hoped for easy and tidy results. Research isn't like that. Every project has its hazards and obstacles. There's rarely anything tidy about gathering information on a narrowed down topic. That's why we've looked at so many strategies. While you won't use them all in every research project, you need to have them in your arsenal just in case your next research adventure turns into a fight for your very life. Who said research is boring?

7.9 For Further Study

Study Guide

1. Summarize for yourself the research strategies covered so far.
2. What is ERIC, what kinds of documents does it provide access to, and what subject areas does it cover best?
3. Where do you find the ERIC database? In what format is the text of most ERIC documents from the early 1990s to the present?
4. What is the Eric Thesaurus?
5. What's the difference between ED and EJ in ERIC?
6. What resources can provide a lot of help in locating government documents?
7. What's the main problem with locating doctoral dissertations? What avenues can you follow to get you hands on one if you want it?
8. What electronic *reference* sources are available at the research library you are using?

Practice with Resources Introduced in this Chapter

For practice with ERIC, see the Assignment below. For some of the other resources listed in this chapter, try these searches:

1. From **http://www.access.gpo.gov/su_docs/fdlp/ec**, go to the link for "Locator Tools and Services." Once there, choose "Browse Topics."
    a. From the A-Z links, find the topic "Social Security Administration," and find the Office of Policy Data. Find out how many people are receiving benefits for the most recent month.
    b. Find the site for the "Central Intelligence Agency" and locate the "World Factbook."
2. For Canadians, or those interested in Canadian things (and who isn't?), go to **http://www.canada.gc.ca/**, choose your language, and enter the site. Choose "Publications and Reports" from the left column.
    a. Look at "Publications by Topic" to find a document for newcomers to Canada on finding a job.
    b. Under the topic related to consumer information, find a document on residential wood heating

3. Go to **http://www.ipl.org/div/subject/browse/law20.40.00/**. From the link related to international documents of governments, find the home page of the parliament of Iceland.

Assignment

1. Do a search for a topic relevant to ERIC using the Thesaurus function, adding at least one keyword to limit your search, and further limiting to ERIC Documents only. List at least 10 relevant documents that you retrieved in your search.
2. Go through each of the cases above and learn what you can.
3. Try out a few of these topics, narrow them, then locate materials in various formats (books, journals, good Web sites). Obviously you won't have time for a lot of in-depth work, but see what you can accomplish in an hour or two:

The Abortion Debate
Anti-Semitism
Causes of World War One
Charlemagne
Confucianism
The Crusades
The Euthanasia Debate
Family Violence
Homelessness
Issues Facing the Modern City
Martin Luther
Moral Development of Children

8

Learning How to Read for Research

It's all very well to amass an enormous bibliography and have all your sources scattered artfully on your desk. But if you're assuming that your essay or research report is now as good as written, you're a couple of sandwiches short of a picnic. Getting the research materials is only half the battle. Now you have to read them and evaluate them. This chapter majors on the joys of reading and note-taking.

8.1 Reading for the Connoisseur and the Glutton

With a tantalizing heading like the one above, you may want to head for the nearest cafeteria. But read on—food for the mind is better than French fries.

Our generation is very big on what is commonly called "escapist fiction." This is the kind of book that makes no claim to be great literature with deep themes but does promise to take you out of yourself and into a far more exciting world.

I, like many librarians, enjoy reading thrillers, spy novels and so on. I've even been known to write and publish such fiction in my spare time. This does get me dubious glances from some people, but I am amazed at how many seemingly sophisticated academics read the same stuff.

The advantage of a thriller is that it gives you a way to escape. You can sit back and let it happen without pondering or analyzing too deeply. Let the skilled thriller writer feed you the adventure until you scream for mercy. Escapist fiction is for gluttons.

I do not, however, call a well-crafted mystery novel "escapist" in the same sense. The writer of this kind of work dares you at every point not only to figure out who did it, but why and how whoever did it did it. In other words, such a writer does not want you to swallow the novel whole (as in a thriller) but to read it with discernment, pausing to think over clues with reserve and intelligence. The well-crafted mystery novel is for connoisseurs.

Where is all this leading? Simply to this basic statement: *Research is not for gluttons.*

Consider the problem you face: You have twenty-five scattered sources and seven Web sites waiting to be read. They comprise 3,423 pages in total. At an average rate of one page every two minutes, this will take you 6,846 minutes to read, or, in more familiar terms, 114.1 hours. If you skip classes for two weeks (or take a vacation from your job) and read 8.15 hours per day, you will have it all read. But wait a minute (even though you have none of these to spare)—I haven't allowed you the time you need to take notes on what you're reading nor to ponder its value. You'd better plan on three weeks.

Before we get too far into the realm of the ridiculous, I think you can see that there is no way you will be able to read and take notes on 3,423 pages for one research project. The approach that works so well for devouring spy novels—gluttonously reading without much thought—is going to sink you when you try to read research materials. There has to be a way to determine what's important and what's a red herring (or a blue elephant).

Let me show you the connoisseur's approach to reading:

8.1.1 Be Ruthless

You may not like what I have to say now, but I do have to say it. *Any book or article you read for research purposes must be used and discarded as quickly as possible.* Forget that the author probably worked long into the night, leaving a weeping spouse and children waiting outside the study door. Forget that for perhaps years the author was utterly consumed by the burden of this topic until it could be rendered into print.

You need information. The source you are reading has information. The problem is that it has too much information that is not relevant to your research topic. Thus you need to use every skill you have to sift quickly through the material you don't need and find the material you do need.

At this point I must warn you not to show this chapter to anyone with an academic title. Such a person may very well burn your copy of *Research Strategies* right in front of you. Professors are purists, and rightly so. They have written one or more theses for which they actually did read all 3,423 pages plus 74,689 more. They got into the hearts and souls of the authors they were reading.

You, on the other hand, are writing a paper that is due, along with two others, in seven days. *Be ruthless.* Read what you need and abandon the rest. It's your only hope.

One big note of caution: I am not urging you to read out of context. You have to read enough of an author's work to have a good idea of his or her main message. It's all very well to be efficient and discerning (the connoisseur) rather than a mindless sponge (the glutton), but be very sure you have grasped not only what the author is saying, but why the author is saying it.

8.1.2 Get to Know the Material without Reading It All

No, this is not permission to do skimpy research. This is an attempt to show you how to zero in on what you need without missing anything important. Here are the steps to take, first for books, then for articles:

Books

> ➢ At the start of the process, have a good look at the title page, preface, foreword, and introduction. A book is not just a series of paragraphs. There is usually a motive and a plan, so the preliminary pages can often give you solid clues as to why the book was written and what it intends to do. Title pages are often ignored because they seem to have so little information on them. But they can be important. Be sure to look at both the title and subtitle, since increasingly titles are there just to look cute, while the real purpose of the book is revealed in the subtitle. Consider these gems:

> *Lifestyle: Conversations with Members of the Unification Church*
> *Passages: Predictable Crises of Adult Life*
> *Sex in the Snow: Canadian Social Values at the End of the Millennium*

> The preface, foreword, or introduction will often tell you what the author is attempting to do in the book. There you can look for a theme, as well as for a description of the approach to the subject and of the material to be covered. Reading a good preface can sometimes give you all the clues you need to get into the really important data.

> ➢ *Second*, check out the table of contents. This table forms the skeleton upon which the body is hung, the keystone that supports the building, the street signs that give meaning to the metropolis, the—but why go on? The point is simply that the table of contents provides you with the

basic structure of the book in its proper order. Here you find the good, the bad, and the useless for your purposes. There was a time when tables of contents provided main headings, subdivisions, and even short paragraph summaries of the main arguments. Now chances are that most chapter headings you see will be cute but relatively uninformative. Still, it is worth your while to check out the table of contents. It may help you zero in on the chapter that you really want. And it gives you a sense of the writer's whole development of the topic.

➢ *Third,* have a look at the index. Indexes can be good, atrocious, or nonexistent. Their real value (when present) lies in their ability to locate specific information when the book itself covers a broader topic. Comparing the indexing with the information in the table of contents can help you greatly by taking you right to the good parts of the book. But beware of two problems:

- Indexes often list many page numbers after each subject heading, forcing you to do a lot of looking up to find what you want. Comparing chapter headings with page numbers in the index might help you speed up the process by locating the most relevant sections.

- When you have located a relevant paragraph through an index, watch out for your natural tendency to take information out of context. Remember that the paragraph you are reading on page 294 was preceded by the 293 pages that came before it.

➢ *Fourth,* be sure to give the book a run-through, even if you are only going to use a part of it. If you fail to do so, you may miss completely the overall intent of the volume and thus misunderstand what you are reading in one portion of it. A run-through includes:

- Reading opening and concluding portions of each chapter to see what the author intended to cover and what he or she concluded.

- Considering the subheadings in the body of each chapter.

- Going over any summary or conclusion chapter at the end of the book.

- Possibly looking up a book review or two if the book is confusing or potentially controversial.

➤ *Fifth*, when it comes to reading the appropriate portion(s) of the book, be a connoisseur of the argumentation, not a glutton who does not evaluate what s/he's eating as long as s/he's got food in front of him or her. There is only one way to read when you are doing research—*by asking constant questions*. Questions are the absolutely most reliable key to good analysis. Ask yourself:

- What is the author saying?

- What point of view or background is the author coming from that might influence what is being said? Thus, what biases do you discern?

- Is the author really dealing with issues or are there some things missing or minimized in the argument?

- Is the evidence presented fairly? Is there enough evidence? Does the evidence support the author's case? Is there counter-evidence that needs to be considered before you automatically buy into the author's argument?

- How do this author's beliefs compare or contrast with other things you've been reading? (Here you should be able to group authors by what they believe so that you can see who supports whom and who opposes whom).

And so on. Don't merely absorb (gluttony). Analyze. Get involved. Ask probing and constant questions of everything you are reading. It will help your research immeasurably. What's more, your questions will help you start preparing your research for the final writing process.

Articles

With a journal article, or an essay within a book, you lack some of the more familiar signposts—tables of contents, indexes, sometimes even subheadings in the text. To add to the problem, the writer may argue a complex point over several pages without stating a conclusion until the last moment. How do you get a grasp of the article's message in short order and make good use of it?

➤ *First*, find an abstract (a summary of the article) if you can locate one quickly. The most generous journals actually provide their own abstracts in the text of their publications. If this is not the case for your article, the article may well be abstracted in a journal database. With a good abstract, you can discern the author's main points and conclusion.

➤ *Second*, watch for key propositions. *Key what???* A **key proposition**, despite its strange name, is a simple concept. *A key proposition is a statement of what the author believes to be true.* Whether or not it is actually true is something for you to discern, but it is what the author believes to be true. Most pieces of expository writing, whether books or journal articles, have several key propositions dotted throughout with, hopefully, a big key proposition at the end of the article. There are two ways in which an author might present key propositions. Some authors start with a question, then present various lines of evidence, then state a key proposition:

Question➔ Evidence➔ Key Proposition

Others start with a key proposition (in the form of a thesis statement), present evidence for it, then re-state the proposition:

Key Proposition (= Thesis) ➔ Evidence➔ Restated Key Proposition

Your task is to identify how your author presents key propositions, then *find them*. Key propositions form the foundation or the skeleton of the article. Everything else is introduction or evidence. With the key propositions identified, you can get to the heart of what the author is trying to say. [Note: The above procedure works just as well with books]

➤ *Third*, check out the author's conclusion at the end of the article carefully. What is the author's bottom line as far as beliefs or final thoughts are concerned? Presumably everything else in the article has some relation to that final statement.

➤ *Fourth*, if the article you are reading still gives you few clues, read the whole thing. There are times when you just have to muddle through, but it won't hurt as much as you think it will. As you go, try to abstract the article for yourself on paper. It will help your understanding, and if you ever have to refer to it again (in a week, by which time you've forgotten you ever read it), you'll be one step ahead.

8.1.3 A Final Word on Analytical Reading

We have been talking hard realities here—too little time and too much to read. Perhaps professors or employers one day will let students work on fewer but larger projects where they have the hours to do the job right. Until that happens, you will need to know how to practice discriminating reading.

Remember that books and journal articles are sources of data. Develop those skills that will help you extract data with the greatest speed and efficiency. But beware of quoting an author out of context because you did not read enough to get the author's overall message.

8.2 Evaluation of Research Resources

Much of what we might call "evaluation" is part of analytical reading—trying to discern what the author is saying and how credible the author's arguments appear to be. But I do want to add something about the overall evaluation process.

Evaluation has to do with determining the following:

➤ The qualifications of the author. The first qualification that comes to mind is how many academic degrees an author has, but that may not be the only measure of qualification. If your family doctor starts writing books about medieval art, all the academic degrees in the world are not going to make her as competent as someone with a degree in medieval art. If an author is writing on a subject area but lacks a clear understanding of that field, the product is going to be shabby.

➤ The biases of the author. Bias is not necessarily a bad thing, because none of us are 100% objective. It may, indeed, be the bias of the author that is most important to you. For example, if you are writing on prejudice against Chinese people in early 19th century San Francisco, reading primary sources by biased people of the time may well make your case. What is important here is that you *identify* the biases of authors so that you can walk into their works with eyes wide open.

➤ The level of opinion as opposed to evidence. Opinion is not fact. Just because you read something in a published work, you can't assume that it's correct. You understand that, I'm sure, but it's good to hear a reminder sometimes. You must always ask, "How do you know that to be the case? Where's your evidence?"

➢ Whether or not the material is relevant to the problem you are addressing. Here you need to take note of the fact that *relevance is not the same thing as quality.* A book or article may be highly relevant yet not up to par by the measures of scholarship. On the other hand, a book or article may be oozing scholarship but really have nothing much to say directly about the issue you are addressing.

A great resource for evaluation clues is **http://www.lib.berkeley.edu/ TeachingLib/Guides/Evaluation.html**

8.3 Note Taking

You may know some of those rare people who never take notes on the data they are discovering in research. Instead, they gather all their books and articles around themselves just before they start writing their first draft, then cite and quote their sources simply by hauling books out of the pile and looking up appropriate passages. Such people, of course, have photographic memories and the organizational skills of Noah loading the ark. Or they are really only using one source for most of their data while occasionally referring to others to cover up the limited nature of their research. Perhaps (heaven forbid), they're writing their research paper out of their heads and using the occasional book or article citation only as some sort of weak signal to the reader that they did some actual research.

For most of us, it's crucial as we read that we distill out the essential things we are going to have to include in our research paper. We don't have the minds nor the stamina to retain everything, unaided by notes, at least not once our research goes beyond four or five sources. Trying to teach someone how to take notes is almost like trying to teach a baby sparrow to fly. Most of what it takes comes from within, not from instructions. I can try to help you by flapping my arms and showing you the motions, but you have to develop the will and skill to soar for yourself.

Generally I recommend taking notes from one source at a time, covering everything in source (book, article, etc.) before moving on to the next one. The alternative is to create blank pages with subject headings on them or separate subject files on your computer, then to record notes from various sources into these subject designations. This latter method is not recommended, because it drags your notes out of their original contexts, thus losing the threads of thought of the authors you are reading. It's better to cover one book or article at a time, keeping all the notes for it in one place.

One of the biggest problems most students face is that they take too many notes that will later go unused. The key to this problem is to have a good research question and preliminary outline as soon as possible in the research process. If you are one of those people who only discerns your outline for the first time while you are proof-reading the final copy of your paper, you have probably wasted a lot of time taking notes that ended up in the round file beside your desk. After all that needless effort, your paper is probably not very good anyway, because its structure was never planned. If, on the other hand, you have a fairly good idea of what you want to accomplish with your research project, you are less likely to take notes on irrelevant information.

Once you have a clear vision how you want your research materials to help you deal with your question, you next have to decide on a note-taking style.

8.3.1 The Determined Photo-Copier

For some students, note taking is easy. Armed with fourteen dollars in dimes, or a charged up copier debit card, they simply photocopy or print everything that looks important, take all 140 copies home, and assemble an essay. Would that most of us could afford this method.

A bit of advice here:

> ➤ If you are using the copier or computer printer, make sure that you have recorded the *author, title, place of publication, publisher and date* for every book or article from which you've made copies or print-offs (*author, title, journal name, volume number, date, and page numbers* for journals). You'd be surprised at how many people I find wandering the library, wayward photocopy in hand, looking desperately for whatever source they took it from.

> ➤ Use a highlight pen on your copies or print-offs as soon as you have made them, while the information is still fresh in your mind. You want to mark the passages that were of the greatest importance to you so that you will not, sometime later, wonder why you made these copies and prints in the first place.

> ➤ Remember that you are at a disadvantage if you copy or print. "Me?" you grin. "I'm the one with fourteen dollars on my debit card. I'll have everything done in a tenth of the time it takes these longhand scribblers and clickety-click keyboarders around here." Yes, but recognize that you have probably interacted with your material at a far more superficial

level than have those "longhand scribblers and clickety-click keyboard-ers." When you go home tonight and try to wade through all 140 print pages, you may find that you've entered a strange and cruel world in which no landmarks make sense to you and the reasons why you printed/copied even half of the stuff totally escape you.

8.3.2 The Note-Book Computer Whiz

With a notebook computer and a portable scanner like the C-Pen or Wizcom QuickLink Pen, you can input large amounts of text without ever photocopy-ing any of it. You can also use voice recognition software (free in Windows under Control Panel→Speech) to read text into a word processor. Inputting is generally not much of a problem, but retrieval is. I regularly ask students what they do with the research notes they're entering into their computer. For many, all they do is print them and then make use of the notes in paper form. If this is the case, the computer is little more than a fast ballpoint. There are some possibilities, however, for making far better use of notes created on your com-puter. If you can identify key words, you can use your word processor "Find" function to locate those words. You can open several windows of material at the same time and compare them right on screen. You can even buy a special-ized scholarly word processing system which will allow you to use advanced file and search functions as well as helping you with the final paper and for-matting your bibliography by whatever style manual you are using.

One word of caution: Because it is often so easy to input notes, you need to be careful that you keep your notes to a minimum. Simply pulling everything you've been reading into computer files is probably counterproductive.

8.3.3 The Quoter

Some still prefer a low-tech approach with paper and pen or, lacking a portable scanner, they are using their own fingers to type material into computer files. Often the plan is to get down information that is verbatim, that is, take direct quotations. There are some advantages to copying material word for word into your notes, and (inevitably) some disadvantages.

Advantages

➢ You won't have to go back to the book or article later on if you need a suitable quotation. It will be right in your notes.

➢ A quotation method can give you greater accuracy, since you have the actual words of your sources. This is especially helpful when a topic is new to you. When you don't fully understand a writer's argument, you can copy a paragraph that states it. Later, when you are more in tune with the subject, the paragraph may make more sense. If you had tried merely to summarize it before you understood the material, you may have misinterpreted the argument and carried that misinterpretation into your notes.

➢ The mere act of copying helps you get to know the material more intimately, since copying demands that you read more slowly and, in fact, that you read each word several times. In understanding, you will be far ahead of the photocopier when your notes are complete.

Disadvantages

➢ The process can become fairly laborious. It's easier to photocopy.

➢ You must be very careful to quote enough to catch the context. Alternatively, you could summarize the context in your notes, then copy directly the portion that is most important to you.

8.3.4 The Summarizer

This person reads a chunk of material, then summarizes it in his or her own words. The point is to condense several pages into a paragraph of notes or a paragraph into a sentence.

Advantages:

➢ This method is quicker than quoting.

➢ The process of summarizing forces you to think about the material and make it your own.

Disadvantages:

➢ The method does not work well if you are dealing with difficult material that is hard to condense.

➢ You will have to go back to your book or journal article if you find later that you need a quotation.

➢ You have to be very careful that you understand the things you are reading. If you misunderstand, you have no way of checking for accuracy later on, other than going back to your source material.

8.3.5 The Paraphraser (not recommended in most cases)

The difference between summarizing and paraphrasing is that the former *condenses* material while the latter *rewrites each sentence in the reader's own words*.

For example, if the original book or article said:

The rate of increase in building costs is rapidly making home ownership impossible for the average middle class family.

a paraphrase might say:

The speed of growth in the cost to build is quickly making owning a home impossible for the average family with a middle income.

whereas a summary might say:

The rising cost of construction is squeezing out middle class would-be home owners. (i.e., an *interpretation* rather than a paraphrase)

With a paraphrase, you can expect that your paragraph of notes will be as long as the book's paragraph, if not longer.

Possible Advantage:

This method can be helpful if you are working through difficult material. Sometimes just the task of rewriting each sentence in your own words makes the writer's meaning clear.

Why, in Most Cases, Paraphrasing is a Bad Idea:

➢ While sometimes recommended by professors, this method leaves you particularly open to a charge of plagiarism (see the end of this chapter), since you are still reproducing the writer's work, thought for thought if not word for word.

➢ In fact, people who paraphrase tend to change far too little of the original to qualify the result as plagiarism-free. Most paraphrasing that I see appearing in research papers is out and out theft of most of the original author's words as well as his/her thoughts.

➢ The method is laborious. Not only do you have to rephrase each sentence, but your notes will be as long as your original source, maybe longer.

So paraphrase only if you need it to explain a piece of writing to yourself. Word to the wise: *Avoid letting paraphrased material appear in an actual research paper you have written. Paraphrased material only puts you at risk. Summarize instead.*

8.3.6 Which Method is Best?

You can use any or all of these methods, except paraphrasing, to advantage. May I suggest that you keep all of them in your toolkit, using each as is appropriate.

8.4 Further Notes on Note-Taking

➢ If you are quoting, use quotation marks in your notes. If the material you are reading turns a page in the middle of your quotation, put a slash mark or some other indicator into your notes to tell you where the page turned in the original. *Always* indicate, at the bottom of the quotation, the page number(s) of the original source you took the quotation from.

➢ If you are summarizing, conscientiously try to work at using your own wording. If you find that your wording is turning out like a clone of the original, then quote directly or photocopy. With summaries, indicate in the margin of the notes the book pages you are summarizing (in case you want to go back to the book later).

➤ If an insight comes to you as you are reading, include it in your notes. Put square brackets around it and end the statement of your insight with a dash and your initials, like this:

[*Schwartzburg agrees with Smith on this point. Does Flutnof?—WB*]

An "insight" is simply anything that occurs to you as you a reading, as, for example, the discovery that this writer agrees or disagrees with someone else, has omitted something, has made a statement that you would like to challenge, has given you a good idea you want to follow up, and so on.

➤ Make sure you leave nothing out of your notes. Give full information on author, title, place, publisher, date, volume number, page numbers, etc. You don't want to have to relocate a book or article you've already read. Chances are someone else will have it by then and you'll never find out what page that key quotation came from. Other than a cold shower, there's nothing as subduing as having to throw out perfectly good notes because you don't have enough information to use them in your bibliography.

8.5 A Gentle Warning about the Horrible Crime of Plagiarism

Just to end the chapter on a cheery note, let me caution you about the academic crime of *plagiarism*. Plagiarism, to put it simply, is passing on someone else's work as your own. The following examples, if they describe your actions, place you very obviously among the guilty. You are plagiarizing if you:

➤ Quote directly from a book, journal, newspaper, friend's essay, etc. without using quotation marks and a note to indicate that the material is not yours;

➤ "Borrow" text from the WWW by copy and paste without indicating the source;

➤ Paraphrase an author, sentence by sentence, without acknowledging the author as the source of the material;

➤ Use a unique idea put forward by an author without indicating the sources of the idea. When you can't find the same idea in two or more independent sources, then it's unique and you have to tell the reader of your research project where the idea came from. (Concepts that are unique to an author need to be acknowledged, while more generally used information does not).

Plagiarism is an academic crime because it is the theft of someone else's creativity, because it gives the impression that someone else's words or ideas are your own, and because most astute professors catch offenders quite easily (even those who skim their papers off the Internet), and then feel hurt that they have been lied to. This often results in anything from a zero for the paper to expulsion from the institution.

8.5.1 Why Get Stressed about Plagiarism?

With easy access to the WWW and to online full text journals, plagiarism is increasing. A lot of students struggle with why plagiarism is such a big deal. We download music all the time, and the WWW is full of free information. What's the difference between downloading a song and downloading text to put into a research paper? The following may provide some answers:

➢ There is a difference between free access and the ability to claim that you are the author of the information you copied from the Net. If I download a cool song, I may "own" it, but I don't claim that I wrote it. If I download text from a freely available source and then neglect to indicate who authored that text, I'm not only using the information, I'm executing a fraud by leading the reader to believe I actually wrote the stuff.

➢ Intellectual property is a big deal in Western society. To be able to write something and put my name on it is something I value. When someone else takes my material and puts his/her name on it, my intellectual property has been stolen.

➢ When you take someone else's words or ideas and pass them off as your own, you rob those words of their power, because there is a connection between the creator of the information and the information itself. To say that a known authority in the field wrote that: _____ (you fill in the blank) is much more powerful than saying or implying that you wrote the same thing. The power of information comes from the authority of the person who authored that information.

> Research writing is a dialogue. As you address your research question, you know that there are other voices out there who have already expressed points of view about possible answers to your question (the sources you are using—books, articles, and so on). Research involves dialoguing with those sources, agreeing with some, disagreeing with others. If you steal text or ideas from those sources and pass them off as your own words or ideas, you kill the dialogue and leave yourself as the only authority on the topic. A prof can see through that sort of thing in an instant. It's much more powerful to write, "Jones has argued _____ but Smith has countered with the argument that _____. In considering Jones' view, it appears that she has neglected to take into account the evidence that _____." Dialogue—That's what it's all about.

8.5.2 About Getting Caught

Just at the time when it's easier than ever to steal electronic text and paste it into your research project, passing it off as your own, *it's easier than ever to get caught.* If you plagiarize an author's unique ideas, chances are your professor already knows what those unique ideas are. But even if you steal text, your professor can catch you very easily.

For material from the WWW, a simple search on a string of text from your paper (using quotation marks) will likely find you out pretty quickly. The same can be done with full text searches in journal databases. For books, both Google Book and Amazon A9 have a lot of electronic full text available for searching.

Even if you take text from a print book or journal not available electronically, you are still at risk. Case in point—I was reading a student paper that just didn't seem right, so I googled a string of text. The source the student was using wasn't available electronically, but the text I googled was in a Web site as a quotation from the print source. Once I knew what hardcopy book had been plagiarized, I got it off the library shelf and tracked down the rest of the massive amount of plagiarism in the paper.

Some institutions are now using plagiarism detection services like Turnitin. Students submit their papers electronically, and the degree of correspondence between those papers and other electronic sources (including their bank of student papers) is analyzed. The professor gets a report.

So it's getting easier to be caught at the plagiarism game. The results are pretty awful. If your professor is really merciful you'll need to rewrite your paper. Normally the paper gets a zero, with no chance for a rewrite. But at many institutions it doesn't stop there. The plagiarism goes on your academic file, you may be given a failing mark, and you could even be suspended or expelled. Overall, plagiarism can look like an easy way to let someone else do your work for you, but the rewards are not worth the penalty.

For a PowerPoint on plagiarism: **http://www.acts.twu.ca/LBR/plagiarism.ppt.**

For an article expanding on my approach to plagiarism, see Badke, William. "Give Plagiarism the Weight It Deserves." *Online* 31.5 (Sep. 2007): 58-60.

8.5.3 International Students and Plagiarism

International students face some unique challenges with the plagiarism issue. In many cultures, information is seen as the property of the community more than it is the property of the individual. In fact, when other people in a community copy or freely use the information of a great scholar, they are honoring that scholar. If information is seen as communal property, using someone else's words or ideas does not appear to be a serious problem.

Yet even in societies where information is communal, it remains wrong to pretend that other people's words or ideas are your own. Even information that belongs to the community still had an author. If you leave the impression that you are the author, you are committing fraud.

Unfortunately, as well, international students who struggle with English are more likely to be caught when then plagiarize than native English speakers. Why? Because the style of English in the plagiarized material is so obviously different from the style of an English as a second language writer. It is not that international students plagiarize more often than domestic students. It is that international student plagiarists are easier to detect.

For a handbook to guide you in every aspect of your academic life as an international student, including plagiarism, see William Badke, *Beyond the Answer Sheet: Academic Success for International Students.* Lincoln, NE: iUniverse.com, 2003.

For more information on and examples of plagiarism see APPENDIX ONE, section A1.5.4.

8.6 For Further Study

Study Guide

1. What's the difference between connoisseur and glutton reading?
2. In what way do you need to "be ruthless" in research reading?
3. What are the four steps to discovering the overall message of a book quickly?
4. When you get to the fifth step (actually reading material you need), explain the best way to go about it.
5. What is an abstract, and how can it help you?
6. What are "key propositions," and how does finding them help the reading process?
7. What's the secret to avoiding the trap of taking too many notes that you will later not use?
8. What are some of the risks for those who take most of their notes by photocopying their sources?
9. What are the advantages and disadvantages of taking notes using the methods of quoting, summarizing and paraphrasing?
10. What are the 4 further instructions the author gives about key elements of note-taking?
11. Define plagiarism and explain why it is such a serious offence. You might want to supplement your knowledge with the following Web sites:

http://library.camden.rutgers.edu/EducationalModule/Plagiarism/
http://www.csub.edu/ssric-trd/howto/plagiarism.htm
http://www.hamilton.edu/writing/style/plagiarism/plagiarism.html

Practice/Assignment

1. How is your reading going? Is it efficient and effective? Go over the suggestions in the first part of this chapter and discover ways in which you can improve your research reading methods.
2. Assess your methods of note taking. Are they working for you? How would you improve them? Do you see ways to improve efficiency by using your computer in note taking?

9

Organizing Your Resources to Write your Paper

"I have seventy-five pages of notes not counting the photocopy I left on the copier and the two pages which I think fell behind my desk. And I've got at least 7 journal articles printed off, but no notes for them. What a mess! How am I ever going to make an essay out of this chaos? Will there ever be meaning to my life?"

Yes, there will. Take heart. There is a way to organize your disastrous jumble of resources or the chaos of notes in your computer, no matter how incomprehensible it now seems to be.

I hesitate whenever I suggest "my" method for organization. What if your mind, heaven forbid, does not correspond with mine? What if I am totally out of touch with the logical categories you most enjoy?

Still, someone has to suggest something. Librarians, even though dull, are undoubtedly logical and thus better equipped than, say, Renaissance painters, to suggest methods of organizing information. I am giving you only one method (with some variations) because throwing too many methods at you can be confusing. If you don't like this approach, ask your favorite professor or another librarian to suggest a better one.

My system can be called a "register method" of resource organization. A "register" is an index list of some sort that enables you to organize data. Consider an auto parts store. The parts are laid out in bins on row after row of shelves. The fact that the water system thermostats are next to the distributor caps that are next to the spark plugs is not nearly as relevant as the fact that each bin has a number on it.

When I walk in and ask for a thermostat for a 1949 Wuzzly Roadster, the parts person does not immediately proceed to the shelves and start looking. He or she opens a parts book or searches a database to find the bin number for that model of thermostat. Then it's an easy task to find the bin with the right number on it and deliver the part to me.

Here's the point of the analogy: The rows of auto parts are your jumbled mess of notes and printouts. The bin numbers are codes you insert into these resources, such as page numbers and other symbols. The parts book or computer index represents an indexed outline by which you can retrieve your notes in a coherent way. This is how it works:

9.1 Your Notes, Photocopies and Printouts

9.1.1 Organizing your Notes

Some people write notes on 3 x 5 or 4 x 6 cards. This is, in my humble opinion, a grave error, compounded by the fact that we live in a computer age. Even an average-sized journal article requires two or three cards, written on both sides to summarize its main points. A book could increase the number of cards to twenty or thirty. Not only is that costly, but you know you're going to lose a least a few cards before your research is done.

If God had meant us to write out notes on cards, he would not have allowed us to invent standard notepaper or computer printers that take standard paper sizes. Does not nature itself tell you that eyes, hands and pens were made for writing boldly on decent sized paper instead of scraping one-sixteenth inch high letters on miniscule cards? Are not computer printers set to standard size paper by default?

Save your note cards for the next part of my system if you wish (though there are better ways), and produce your notes (if you are using print or printing computer notes) on normal paper, hole-punching them and keeping them together in a binder. Be sure, however, to follow a consistent method. As you begin notes on each book or article, be very certain that you include full bibliographical information in the notes (author, title, place, publisher, date, volume number, and page numbers).

When you have completed your notes for a particular item (even if those notes are ten pages long), simply leave a few lines blank, then start notes on your next book or article, being sure again to enter full bibliographical information first. (If you are using a computer, see the alternatives below.)

One of the important things you need to do is *number the pages of your notes consecutively*. If you have fifty pages of notes on ten pages, then number your note pages from one to fifty. (If using a computer, see below). If you have photocopies or journal article printouts, put them in the right places in your notes and number them along with the notes, even if you end up with 150 pages numbered consecutively.

9.1.2 Options for Notes Using a Computer

Some people prefer to print their digital notes onto paper. In this case, the computer is just an input device, and notes are handled as above.

If you are planning to retain your notes in their electronic format, you need to determine how you want to set them up for easy retrieval of the information you need. Unless you have a note organization program, it's probably best to put all your notes into one file so that you can search them with only one search rather than several. *Make sure you back up your information constantly if it's all in one file. You'd hate to lose the whole thing.*

Your word processor's "find" function (in the "edit" menu) will become a retrieval tool, though in the organizing process you may need to input some codes (see below).

9.2 Your Bibliography

As you gather sources, you have to keep track of them, including enough bibliographical information so that you won't need to go on a desperate search for a lost date or volume number when you start writing your paper. The best resource for this task is a bibliographic manager like RefWorks, EndNote or the free online Zotero (See Chapter 7 for explanation of these tools).

Here's the minimal information you need to include for a proper citation:

Book—author, title, city of publication, publisher, date.
Journal Article—author and title of article, journal title, volume number, date (e.g., (January 1999) or (2000)), and page numbers where the article is found.
Journal Article from an Electronic Periodical Database—everything listed under Journal Article above plus the date you accessed the article, and either the persistent link or the DOI, depending on what bibliographical style you are using. For example:

Badke, William. "Give Plagiarism the Weight It Deserves." Online 31.5 (Sep. 2007): 58-60. Academic Search Premier. EBSCO. [Library name], [City], [State abbreviation]. 26 October 2007. <https://ezproxy.student.twu.ca/login?url=http://search.ebscohost.com/login.aspx?direct=true&db=aph&AN=26378977&site=ehost-live>.

Conley, D., Pfeiffera, K. M., & Velez, M. (2007). Explaining sibling differences in achievement and behavioral outcomes: The importance of within—and between-family factors. Social Science Research, 36(3), 1087-1104. doi:10.1016/j.ssresearch.2006.09.002

Essay in a Book—author and title of essay, title of book, editor of book, city of publication, publisher, date, and page numbers where the essay is found.
Reference Book Article—title of article, author if given (often abbreviation of author name is given at the end of the article), title of reference book, edition of reference book; and (sometimes) city of publication, publisher, date.
Web site—author (if given), title, publisher (if given), Internet address (URL), and date you most recently accessed the information.

9.3 Your Subject Index

Note taking and printout gathering is easy. Retrieval is hard. The biggest problem most students face is that they've ended up with many pages of notes and printouts, but now that they want to write the research paper, they can't retrieve the data they need from these resources.

Virtually anyone, even a seasoned author, gets writing anxiety—that moment when you are finally staring at a blank computer screen (with the cursor blinking in taunting fashion) or a blank piece of paper, and your mind tells you that this essay will never happen. You may have written brilliant works in the past (or not), but this one simply will never see the light of day. The fear quotient is tremendous.

Now, imagine that you have the further problems that your notes are a mess, you're not sure you did enough research, and you can't find even the data you remember noting down. Writing anxiety now becomes writing crisis. The only way to save yourself all this *angst* is to get organized before you write.

Sure, I know you're thinking, "My paper is due in 3 hours. I don't have time to get organized."

My response is that *you don't have time NOT to get organized.*

Let me suggest a method that will break the back of writing anxiety and actually save you time in the long run. Here are the steps:

➤ Take a good-sized piece of paper and write your preliminary outline on it, leaving lots of space between each heading or subheading. (You *do* have a preliminary outline, don't you? If not, you've probably already wasted a lot of time researching things that aren't relevant to your topic, which is why your barely started paper is due in three hours.)

➤ Determine a symbol to represent each heading or subheading. These symbols could be the letters and numbers used in your outline (I, A, 1, a, etc.) or special symbols not normally used in written work: #, $ % +, etc.

➤ If you are working with notes in paper form, read through your notes. Every time you discover data that is relevant to one of your headings in your outline, write the location (page number of notes) under that heading. In your notes, insert your symbol so that you can find the exact location of the data. (If this is confusing, see the example below.)

➤ If you are working with computer files, type the symbols (%, #. %, or whatever) into the spots in your online file that are relevant to sections of your outline. The "find" function under "edit" in your word processor can then locate any symbol and its relevant notes any time you need them. *Just remember to insert a space after the symbol so that the "find" function can actually find it.*

For example:

% Darwin's approach to natural selection made it possible … etc.

Thus, with this exercise of organization, you cross-reference your notes with your outline so that you can retrieve the relevant notes as you write your paper. The outline may then look something like this:

The Limits of Behaviorism: *Walden Two* in Perspective
I. An Introduction to Behaviorism
4 17 [page numbers only needed if your notes are in print; for computer files, only the symbol # is necessary].

II. B.F. Skinner's *Walden Two*
$ 3, 18, 3

III. *Walden Two* as a Demonstration of the Limits of Behaviorism
% 6, 12, 14-17

In the above example, note that my symbols are #, $ and %. These symbols will also be inserted in the appropriate places in the printed notes or computer files for easy retrieval of data.

Why go to all this trouble? Simply because it saves time and alleviates writing anxiety. Consider this awful alternative: You begin writing your paper and get to heading number one: "An Introduction to Behaviorism." Now you have to do a keyword search with your find function (with unpredictable results) or rummage through all forty-seven pages of your printed notes, looking for material on this aspect. Having found your material and written this section of your paper, you come to your second roadblock: the next heading—"B.F. Skinner's *Walden Two*." Now you have to go through your notes again, for a second desperate search for relevant information. Then comes heading number three, and the whole nasty quest starts over again. In the process, you will have plowed through all your notes three times and recreated your writing anxiety three times.

Thus, setting up an index to your notes before you start writing saves you having to re-read your material every time you start a new section of your paper. Besides, you are left with a warm and comforting sense that you actually know where you are going before you start. When was the last time you had a feeling like that?

9.4 Indexing your Notes for Larger Assignments

There may well come a time when you are asked to produce a really large research paper like a thesis or dissertation. Now the process of note organization becomes crucial, because retrieval is much more complicated.

In general, the procedures I've outlined above work just as well on longer papers as they do on shorter ones. True, your outline itself may be several pages long, and you may have to modify what symbols you use to identify headings, but the same principle still operates—your goal is to cross-reference outline headings to your notes so that as you write the various parts of your paper you can retrieve the research data you need.

A few tips for larger projects (beyond the obvious that you should always back up your files):

➢ Do your indexing as you are going along in your research rather than waiting to the end and being faced with the task of indexing a massive computer file or dozens (even hundreds) of printed pages of notes.

➢ Make especially sure that you are managing your bibliography well. The larger the bibliography, the more the risk of losing things. Here a bibliographic manager is well worth the effort it takes to make it your friend.

➢ If your preliminary outline should change as you are going through the research process, don't panic. Go back over what you've already indexed and transfer your old indexing, as best you can, to the new outline. Sometimes this will mean going back over your notes again and doing some re-indexing.

Research may be fun, but nobody said it was easy. Come to think of it, though, isn't the challenge what makes it so much fun?

9.5 For Further Study

Study Guide

1. Write out an explanation of the "register method" of note organization, including a good description of each of the parts.
2. If note taking and doing printouts are easy, what is hard? Why?
3. In using a computer as your note taking device, what options do you have for retrieval?
4. Why go to all this trouble to organize notes and establish retrieval procedures?

Practice/Assignment

Assess your past method(s) of note organization. Would the register method work for you? Can you think of another method that you'd prefer?

10

Tips on Research Writing

Research doesn't mean much if the presentation of your results is flawed. The kiss of death for any project is to have your research paper returned with the comment: "Excellent bibliography, but your argument could have been developed more clearly."

Two problems stand out as the most common roadblocks in the writing process: Getting your outline straight and writing persuasively. Let's deal with each in turn.

10.1 The Final Outline

Earlier, I argued that you need to have a preliminary outline pretty much from the beginning of the research process to act as a guide for the gathering of resources. In the early stages, organizing your outline is not crucial, but eventually you are going to have to structure it in a final form. Outlining is a major problem in any research presentation. If you are attempting (in fear, no doubt) a thesis or dissertation, the problem only compounds itself.

Let's visualize what we're dealing with first, then look at some possible solutions. The reason why the outline is so troublesome is that people receive information in sequence rather than absorbing all of the facts at the same time. Simply because a twenty page paper may take fifteen minutes to read means that some information must be presented before other information is given.

Let's look at it another way. Putting forward an argument (that is, the statement of a response to your research question) is like building a house. You have to lay the foundation before you can move to the upper stories. Everything you build rests upon whatever you've already laid down.

Perhaps the best way to learn outlining technique is to look at specific steps and see these illustrated with specific examples.

10.1.1 Step One: The Research Question

As we have seen, the first step toward putting together even a preliminary outline is figuring out what issue you want to deal with. This involves narrowing your topic and stating a *single* research question. For our purposes, let's choose the topic of "Burnout in the Workplace." Our narrower focus will be "preventing burnout," and our research question is, "How can today's office worker best resist burnout in the workplace?"

10.1.2 Step Two: Preliminary Outline Headings

Now you need to assess your question to determine what data you are going to need to answer it. For our example, presumably you'll need an introduction to burnout, explaining what it is and raising the issue that there must be means to resist it. You might, as well, assume that resisting this problem will involve recognizing the signs of burnout and taking some counter-measures to overcome those signs or to prevent them happening in the first place. Thus your preliminary outline has three possible headings already: Knowing the Signs of Approaching Burnout, Counter-measures, and An Introduction to the Problem of Burnout.

10.1.3 Step Three: Organizing the Headings

Organizing the outline in sequence is usually the hardest part. What you want is a logical order that is helpful to the reader. Above all, you want to avoid the impression that your paper lacks direction or that the direction it is taking is strange and hard to justify. A good outline should not be all that noticeable because your goal is to take the reader from introduction to conclusion as comfortably as possible.

A Few Tips

> ➢ Get general and introductory matters out of the way first. Just as you needed a working knowledge of the topic when you started your research, you now need to give your reader a similar working knowledge,

including background information and a clear statement of the question you're dealing with. In the case of our burnout example, you would probably have to define burnout, demonstrate what a problem it is, then ask what things could be done to resist burnout in the workplace.

➢ Look for a natural order to your headings, if you can find it. In our burnout example, it seems more natural to discuss first the need to recognize the signs of burnout and *then* to consider possible counter-measures to resist burnout (i.e., knowledge before action seems like a natural order).

➢ Here are some other possibilities:

- In a historically-oriented paper (e.g., "The Early Conquests of Alexander the Great"), you might simply want to move the paper along chronologically.

- In an analysis of issues related to a topic, you can follow an ascending or climactic order, looking at smaller factors or arguments first, then moving up to the more crucial factors. Your last section could begin,

"The most serious difficulty with_____, however, is_____."

Ascending or climactic order adds power to a paper by leading the reader into increasing tension, much like an action movie builds to a climax. Resist giving away the most exciting parts of your paper early on—if you use up the good stuff too soon, you'll have little left to keep the reader interested in the rest of what you have to say.

- You need to include all relevant points of view on an issue, not just the one you support. When a research project ignores opposing arguments, the reader feels cheated, and the case you are making is weakened, not strengthened. An argument that pays no attention to other voices will not stand up to a challenge.

Comparing and Contrasting

If you are comparing or contrasting two or more viewpoints, there are basically two ways to go about it. Now's a good time to get your wits about you, so go have some coffee or take a walk, then read on

If the two views you are discussing are relatively simple to explain and analyze, try a *longitudinal method* by which you discuss all aspects of view A and then moved on to discuss all aspects of view B. Suppose, for example, you were dealing with two views on the issue of human cloning—**Go Ahead** and **Wait a Minute: What Do You Think You're Doing?**

Your outline might look like this:

I. Introduction to Human Cloning
II. The Go Ahead Position
    A. All Science is Legitimate.
    B. We Can Trust Scientists Not To Put Us At Risk.
    C. The Benefits of Having Clones Outweigh The Risks.
III. The Wait A Minute Position
    A. Is all Science Legitimate?
    B. Can We Trust Scientists Not To Put Us At Risk?
    C. Do The Benefits Outweigh The Risks?
IV. Conclusion

You can see that we are presenting one position in total, then the other, using our discussion of the second position as a base to deal with the arguments against the first. Thus the Go Ahead Position will be covered as objectively as possible. The analysis will come with the Wait a Minute Position.

But suppose that the arguments are getting complicated, and you're afraid your reader will have forgotten what the first position said about the legitimacy of science before you have time to discuss it in the second position. In such a complex situation, you'll need a *cross-sectional approach*, which deals with both sides of each sub-topic in turn:

I. Introduction to Human Cloning
II. Is All Science Legitimate?
    A. Yes
    B. Maybe not
III. Can We Trust The Scientists?
    A. Yes
    B. Not always
IV. Do the Benefits of Having Clones Outweigh the Risks?
    A. Yes
    B. Maybe not
V. Conclusion

Now you have the chance to deal with both sides of each issue in turn. By the time you get to your conclusion, your reader should have a cumulative understanding of the issues and of the reasons for your position.

A couple of other tips:

> Avoid stringing out a list of 7 or more headings without subheadings, because this tends to damage the unity and coherence of your paper (just like leading someone down a winding path creates more confusion than guiding the same person down a short city block with sights to see on all sides). How do you cover the ground without multiplying your outline's headings? You do it by having a few main headings and adding subheadings to them. Thus you *group* your points, arguments, etc. under 3 to 5 main categories and let subheadings pick up the detail. This makes a tighter structure that has more of a chance of achieving unity in the paper. See the outlines above for examples of useful ways to do this.

> Attempt objectivity at the beginning and do your analysis later. Here I need to get on a soapbox for a few moments:

Why does objectivity come before analysis? Because every view needs to be heard before you criticize it. Suppose you are doing a paper on the well known (at least to me, since I created him) social scientist Horace Q. Blowhard, who has the audacity to argue that the death penalty should be instituted for traffic offenses in order to restore public order. Your paper, entitled "Why Don't You Stand In Front of *My* Car, Horace?" intends to rip the man to shreds. But how can you do this most effectively?

If you are still unclear about the fine points of intellectual maturity, you may want to begin you paper with the words, "Horace Q. Blowhard truly lives up to his name. If there were ever a reason for tar and feathers, Horace (no friend of yours or mine) would be it." From here, your outline would be:

I. Condemnation of Blowhard
II. Some of the Most Vile of his Views
III. Concluding condemnation.

But this is utterly the wrong approach. O ye contenders for justice and all for which it stands, halt and listen up: *No one deserves to be torched verbally or in print before he or she has been given a fair and objective hearing.* Not even Horace Q. Blowhard.

I know what you're thinking now—when did true objectivity ever exist? All of us are subjective, so why not just state our views without worrying about truth and fairness to other viewpoints? Why try to give anyone an objective hearing? My answer is that, while this is neither the time nor the place to get into the murky depths of Postmodernism, all of us know that it's possible to hear someone, understand that person and treat that person's views fairly. Sure, our presuppositions will get in the way to some extent, but our goal still needs to be to understand the positions of others as best we can *before* we level either praise or crushing criticism. A good measure of objectivity is still possible for most of us.

Devastating attacks do not come before we have explained the position of our opponents. They come after, when both you and the reader have enough knowledge of the opposing position to determine whether you are launching the right missiles. Anything less than this is poor sportsmanship, bad form, bigotry, whatever you want to call it. Mature writing makes sure every view has been heard fairly before it is analyzed.

10.2 Some Tips on Research Writing

10.2.1 Introduce your paper well

Introductions serve two purposes:

> ➢ They give you a chance to provide your reader with a working knowledge of your topic.

> ➢ They let you state your (*single*) research question.

One thing to avoid here is the temptation to multiply your research questions along the lines of:

"Why, then, did Skinner write *Walden Two?* Did he indeed believe that he could create Utopia with the methodology of behaviorism? Was he blind to the problems in his approach? Did he later change his mind?"

What you've done is create a shotgun blast heard around the world. Your reader has no idea what your real goal is because you have so many of them. The paper itself will be as superficial and as scattered as your introduction. Keep your introduction lean if not mean.

Sometimes a real life illustration is helpful to get the topic going. For example, if you are doing a paper on a historical figure, you might want to begin with an anecdote from that person's life that typifies what you want to say about him/her. Beyond that, stick with the purposes of an introduction—to provide a working knowledge and to state your research question.

10.2.2 Be focused at all times

There is something almost magic about a successful research paper. If you have a solid, narrowly-focused, analytical research question, you can pretty much see in your mind's eye the problem to be addressed. If you have a well-structured outline, you can envision the path through the paper to a conclusion before you even start writing it. Don't begin writing the paper until everything comes into focus and you have that "Aha" experience that tells you that you know exactly what you plan to do. If it's all fuzzy in your mind, it will remain fuzzy through the writing process, and the product will be fuzzy too (a triple fuzzy can't be a good thing).

If you keep the narrow focus on what you are doing, magic will happen.

10.2.3 Always describe before you analyze.

You thought I had long since fallen off my soapbox. Don't worry. I won't bring it up again. But do it. Your writing will look more mature.

10.2.4 Avoid ridicule.

When you disagree with a certain author or viewpoint, you need to maintain a level of respect and decorum. Your opponent is not a "moron," "idiot," "stupid" or "useless." (Believe it or not, I've seen all of these terms in student papers). This kind of language reminds me of an elementary schoolyard with two kids arguing about an issue until one of them runs out of ideas and says, "Oh yeah? Well, I think you're stupid." Ridicule is the lowest form of argument. It reveals immaturity and a lack of ability to address the issues in an intelligent manner. Such language only reflects badly on you.

10.2.5 Be logical.

By this, I mean that, whenever you are traveling along a certain train of thought, make sure your reader is in the caboose behind you. Don't flit around. Don't jump to another track without warning. Always remember that you are writing for someone who doesn't know where you're going. Lead your reader along gently, step by step. Stay on track. For example, when you move on to a new area of discussion, use a transitional phrase such as, "Turning to the issue of ..."

Having a clear sense of your research question and outline is a great help here. If you have a single focus for your paper and understand the steps you need to take from question to solution, it's easier to help your reader stay with you. To make sure you're really on track, ask yourself for each paragraph in your paper:

> ➢ Is this paragraph in the right place in my paper (i.e., does it match the heading it's under)?

> ➢ Does this paragraph contribute to the solution for my research question?

There are times when I come across a research paper with a "bulge" in it. What's a bulge? It's a body of information that has little relationship to the paper topic. How did it get there? The researcher worked for a long time on something that, as it turned out, didn't really relate to the final paper. But no one wants to admit a big waste of time, so the researcher simply plugged the less-than-relevant material into the paper anyway. This turned what might have been a lean and mean research essay into an ugly project with an unsightly bulge in the middle of it. The poor reader is left to figure out what the bulge has to do with anything else.

10.2.6 Be explicit.

I don't know how many students there are out there (good, otherwise intelligent, students) who believe in ESP. They assume that their professors can read their every thought even it is never expressed. Thus we get a gem that looks something like this:

> "In looking at the issues of Nicea, we must focus of the Arian Debate. The facts are well known and thus we move to the specific role of the famous Athansius in dealing with ..."

What's a Nicea? What's an Arian Debate? Who's Athanasius and, if he's so famous, why have I never heard of him? If you don't explain yourself clearly throughout, your reader has no idea whether you know what you're writing about either.

10.2.7 Aim for clear writing rather than erudition.

The mark of an educated person is not the length of words and sentences used but *the ability to communicate complicated information in plain language.* Be concise. Say what you mean. Avoid like the plague every long word where a shorter word would work as well. Try never to be ambiguous.

10.2.8 Watch out for flawed arguments.

These include:

> *Misrepresenting authorities.* If you are appealing to someone's work as support for your argument, be very sure that you represent that person accurately. Don't quote out of context, suppress information that would give a more honest picture, or do anything similar. This sort of misrepresentation is best left to the tabloid newspapers.

> *Arguments from origins.* Just because a viewpoint arose from a dubious source, it does not necessarily mean that it's wrong. If a nasty government that exploits the poor of its nation comes up with a wonderful invention to help end famine in the world, is the invention of no value simply because the government it came from is exploitive? Of course not. Those who know about such things are going to have to examine this invention and make their own assessment, regardless of its origin. Similarly, we can't always assess the value of an idea by considering the person who suggested it. While it might seem legitimate to doubt the advice on family unity put forward by someone who has been divorced seven times, you have to look at the person's material itself. The concepts may be sound even though the author does not exemplify them.

> *Arguments from insufficient evidence.* I am constantly amazed at the way some researchers skip over weighty problems without making their case. They use expressions like, "It is obvious that ..." or "Such a view is unacceptable today ..." or "In my opinion ..." even though

much more effort is needed to convince the reader that it really is obvious or unacceptable. My reaction when I see statements without sufficient evidence is to assume one of three things: the writer hasn't done enough research to discover that a controversy exists, the writer has no evidence to offer and is trying to bluff through the problem, or the writer is vain enough to believe that his/her mere opinion is all any reader needs in order to be convinced.

How much evidence is sufficient? Enough to be convincing. When you write a research paper or report, you need to imagine a reader who is slightly hostile, who is *not* prepared to believe you. Then you must present enough support for your argument that your hostile reader will at least say, "Well, you make a good case." You don't need absolute proof, just enough evidence to get your reader to take your view seriously.

If you don't have the evidence to do this, then you will have to be a lot more humble about sharing your views. Admit that evidence is scarce and that, therefore, any position you are taking on the matter is tentative.

Sometimes, the evidence is not available at all. If that's the case, admit it. Write something like, "There continues to be much debate over this issue, and no consensus seems possible until more evidence is found." (Do not suicidally write: "I can't understand this issue, so I haven't made up my mind.")

10.2.9 Know when to quote and when not to quote

You should quote:

> ➤ When you want to back up your view with that of a prominent scholar who agrees with you.

> ➤ When something someone has written is catchy or memorable in its wording. For example, Bruno S. Frey, in his book, *Dealing with Terrorism: Stick or Carrot,* gives the following clear analysis of the difference between deterrence and brute force:

> "Deterrence is not necessarily the same as using brute force. Deterrence involves the *threat* of damage to an adversary. It would be most successful if it were possible not to actually carry it out." (p. 28)

> In a few short sentences, he explains a crucial distinction in such a way that little more needs to be said.

You should not, however, quote:

➤ When you can say it just as well in your own words.

➤ When the material you want to quote is over 5 or 6 lines long (unless it is absolutely crucial in its original wording and is necessary for the central theme of your paper).

➤ When you already have a quotation every page or two in your essay. You don't want to fill your paper with quotations. Your reader primarily wants your wisdom, not that of everyone else.

10.2.10 Know some basic Rules for Quotations.

Make it a habit to present your own material first, then back it up with a quotation. Quotations should not normally be used to present new data. Here the issue is one of authority. Every time you present new data with a quotation, you are deferring to the authority of your source. That knocks the wind out of your own authority as an author. Let's put it this way: *Whose paper is it?* It's yours. Stand on your own two feet and make your own statements. Quotations are for backup and support.

Thus the pattern you should use is something like this: In your own words present some data or a viewpoint, then follow up with something like "As Joseph Schwartz has argued …", then quote from Schwartz in support of your data or viewpoint. Even if you are just presenting the views of someone (e.g., B.F. Skinner), present those views in your own words first, then if you need to, follow up with a quotation from Skinner that summarizes his position well.

Never, never, never, ever write a paper that strings together long quotations interspersed with only a few lines of commentary by you. Such papers are doomed, since your professor knows that her ten-year-old could paste together the same quotations just as well. A research paper is supposed to be predominantly a presentation of material in your own words, showing that your can present data and use that data analytically to answer an important question. Use quotations sparingly, merely as support for what you are saying.

If you have a book or article that quotes another source, and you want to use that quotation, the rule is to find the original source that the quotation came from and quote that source directly. Until you go back to the original source, you can't know for sure whether the quotation was accurate or quoted in its proper context was. Only if you can't find the original source should you use the book or article in which you found the quotation. Even then, you need to indicate what you are doing:

3

Raymond Sludge, *The Red Rose,* 47, as quoted in Horace Roebuck, "Roses are Forever," *Flower Journal* 42 (May 2000): 76.

But think twice before you use this option. Some professors will punish you for doing so (and, of course, professors are the ones with all the power).

10.2.11 Know the uses of footnotes/endnotes/citations.

These days, most students are using short forms of citations (e.g., Jones, 241) instead of the more traditional footnotes and endnotes. In this case, only the first of the purposes below is going to interest you. But don't forget that you can still add footnotes related to the other purposes below, even when you're using a short citation method.

The purposes of Footnotes/Endnotes/Citations include:

> ➢ Citing works you have quoted or borrowed ideas from. Most students are aware that direct quotations need to be noted/cited. But you need also to footnote borrowed ideas if they are relatively unique. Here's a (perhaps simplistic but helpful) rule of thumb: If you use an idea that you can only find in one or two of your sources, it's better to cite the source(s). If the material is found in three or more sources and you can't see that these are borrowing their idea from a single source in the past, don't bother with a note/citation.

> ➢ Stating further bibliography for the reader who may be interested in pursuing the matter. This procedure, which might look a bit tedious, shows the extent of your research and could earn you appreciation from the reader (and a higher grade if the reader is a professor). Even if you are using a short citation format in the body of your paper, you can still add further bibliography as a footnote.

> ➢ Citing sources that agree with your position. This is especially useful if you know you've gone out on a limb and you suspect your professor is ready to cut it off at the trunk. The support of five other scholars who agree with you may not prove your case, but at least it shows that you are not a flake. Begin this type of footnote/endnote with something like: "So too Steven Johnson, [etc.]" or "This position is also held by …"

> ➢ Defending a certain position against possible objections. Here you are not sure someone will object to what you are saying, but you see a

potential flaw in the argument. It's better for you to point out the problem yourself and respond to it before your reader can raise it as an issue. A format for this could begin, "It might be objected that … but [then give your response to the possible objection]." This type of note shows your reader that you are not trying to present a whitewash with only your side represented. If, however, you find that the possible objection you are responding to is important for the whole thrust of your paper, include it in the actual text of your paper. Notes are for additional or less relevant material.

> Dealing with a related side issue that might spoil the flow of the essay itself if it were to appear in the text. This use is rare, but you may want to add to the depth of your paper in this way. Be careful, though, that you don't make the multiplying of notes a habit. I once spoke with a world famous scholar who admitted to me that he had a problem with his use of notes. I refrained from grinning only because I'm a polite librarian. One of this scholar's most celebrated works was published as two equal length volumes. The first volume was the text of his book and the second was his endnotes. I'd say he has a serious problem (though his notes are often fascinating). Avoid having the same difficulty yourself.

10.2.12 Watch your conclusions.

A good conclusion briefly summarizes the main focus of your paper and makes your final position clear. Avoid flowery, sentimental, or overly long conclusions. Say what you need to say and end it mercifully. In general, half a page at the end of a fifteen page paper is more than enough.

10.2.13 Give your final paper a professional look.

Your final project should avoid typographical or spelling errors (use your spell-checker). Find out what style manual your institution is using, and follow it rigorously for title page, outline page, page format, bibliography, etc. With bibliographies, make sure you follow the format rules you've been given. If you haven't been given any, then choose a style manual and follow it (See Appendix A for more on style).

You may be using a bibliographic manager like EndNote or RefWorks that has a bibliography generating function. While this is a big help, remember that no bibliography generator is foolproof. You will have to troubleshoot everything. The best way to do this is to have a crib sheet for your style (a list of the most common examples of form—books, articles, web pages, etc.) and compare it with the bibliography that you've generated, fixing things as needed.

Word to the wise—Professors tend to assume that a sloppy product is evidence of a sloppy mind.

Research can be exciting, even fun.

FUN??? Yes, as long as you see the path of discovery as an adventure. Research can be done well by virtually anyone, no matter what your initial ability may have been. I trust that I have introduced you to sufficient strategies so that you can develop your skills to do first class work. The next stage is up to you.

10.3 For Further Study

Study Guide

1. What are the three steps to take in first establishing an outline?
2. In a research paper or report, what should you cover first?
3. Explain the longitudinal and cross-sectional approach to outlining discussion of more than one view on an issue. Try each method with the following outline elements:

Topic: Physician Assisted Suicide
The points of view: Seeing it as a beneficial aid to sufferers and Seeing it as wrong morally.
The subsections under each view—The problem of unbearable suffering, the wishes of the patient, the risk that we are playing God.

4. What are the two purposes of introductions?
5. Why describe before you analyze?
6. What are some things to remember if you want your paper/report to flow logically so that your reader can follow it?
7. What's a "bulge" in a paper or report?
8. What is the mark of an educated person?
9. Explain types of flawed argumentation.
10. When should you not use quotations? Do you agree with the author's position that your quotations should be few? Why or why not?

11. Why would you use "notes" in your research paper/report?
12. What should you avoid in a conclusion?

Practice/Assignment

Take a paper you have recently done and run it by the suggestions in this chapter. What should you change?

APPENDIX ONE—
A Research Paper Clinic: More Tips
and Troubleshooting for Development
of Great Research Papers

[The following chapter was created for a seminar on research paper writing. It supplements the book *Research Strategies,* but in some cases overlaps with it. If you experience a measure of déjà vu while reading the Appendix, be thankful that you've been given a chance to see a summary, with enhanced examples, of the essay preparation hints discussed in the body of this book. Or use it on its own as a mini-workshop.]

A1.1 Research Questions

A1.1.1 Why Most Research Papers Miss the Target

You have likely been trained to see a research paper as a way to force you to read a lot of material from many sources, then report on what you have read, covering whatever subject you have been given with as much depth as space will allow.

Thus, a research paper on the causes of World War I would begin with a brief history of the events leading to this war, then would list several causes, and would perhaps conclude with a statement that war is bad, and we should watch for warning signs so we can prevent war in the future. What would you say your research paper is about? "It's about the causes of World War I," you'd reply, looking at me strangely. You've read all about those causes in various books and magazines. You've put that material together (that is, you synthesized it), and you've written a paper explaining the causes.

But your paper missed the target entirely. You see, a research paper is not supposed to be *about* anything. Please understand this. If you were writing a genuine research paper, and I asked you, "What is your paper about?" you should be able to answer, "It's about nothing." That response, of course, would result in some questions: *"What do you mean, 'It's about nothing?' Does this mean there's no a topic? Are we in an episode of Seinfeld?"*

Certainly, you have a topic. The problem is that my question, "What is your paper about?" is wrongheaded. It assumes that a research paper is intended to explain a certain topic, using resources that you have studied. That's a false assumption. Studying up on a topic and compiling data about it is not research at all.

What, then, is the point of a research paper?

A research paper seeks to use data from various resources to answer a question or to solve a problem.

Data in this case is not an end in itself but a *means*, a *tool*. Research does not result merely in explanation of a topic. It is a problem-solving exercise that takes data from various sources and analyzes it to help you answer a burning question.

A1.1.2 Getting Focused by Asking the Right Question

If you are merely reporting on what you have read, then you don't have to worry about the purpose of your paper. Your purpose is to explain to your reader everything you know about your topic.

But if you are in search of the answer to a question, you're not really interested in knowing everything about a topic, only what is relevant. Sure, you will do a background study to make sure you understand the issues involved. But your data will become selective, because what you really need to know is *only that portion of the data which can help you answer the question.*

EXAMPLE:

Instead of describing the causes of World War I, find a controversy that can become a research question. For example, it is often argued that the murder of Archduke Ferdinand was the chief cause of World War I. Your initial research tells you that this is an overly simple explanation. True, this particular assassination did lead to a series of events that began the War, but lots of people are murdered every year without the events turning into a war. Thus you become interested in answering a question like this one: *Why did the murder of Archduke Ferdinand become the flashpoint that led to WWI?*

There are several assumptions here to test out:

➢ This was no ordinary murder.

➢ The murder must have meant something more to the various sides than is apparent.

➢ There must have been a background to this particular murder so that the sides that created a war out of it knew immediately what the murder meant.

I think that in all my teaching of research skills I use one word more often than any other—"Focus." Most people approaching the research task are facing a crisis of lack of proper focus. This is what causes the anxiety, the false view that research is tedious, the shabby research papers and the punishment from the professors who have to read them. Focus, focus, focus. The more your project forms a clear, narrow and single-minded image in your head, the better off you are.

This is where the research question comes in (or thesis statement if you want to go that route). It identifies the research problem and gives you the direction your research needs to take to solve it. The research question, along with a preliminary outline, provides you with a roadmap to success for any project. But a badly constructed question will mess you up every time.

Back in Chapter Two we looked at examples of bad and ugly questions. Let's pick up on those, see what they look like, and learn how to fix them. In each case, we'll define what is good, bad and ugly, look at examples, then suggest some fixes:

A1.1.3 The Question that Isn't There

Questions that aren't there aren't necessarily projects without questions. It's just that the questions don't lead to real research. These are the projects that simply compile information on a topic, then report on it. As such, gathering information is an end in itself, so there is no problem to solve.

Definition of Good—The project not only has a question, but that question leads to a problem-solving exercise in which information is a tool, not an end in itself.

Definition of Bad—The project has a fairly narrow topic but the question is merely informational in its goal.

Definition of Ugly—The project not only merely gathers information, but is itself a survey of a broad subject area without any question to answer.

Examples of Bad and their Fixes:

"What were the events of August 1914 that led to the start of the First World War?"
Fix it by asking: *"Was the assassination of Archduke Ferdinand really as significant a cause of WWI as many scholars assume?"*

"What foods are good sources of low fat protein?"
Fix it by asking: *"Among the top three diet plans, which is the most likely to offer success for long term weight loss?"*

"Who are the Taliban?"
Fix it by asking: *"Is the UN's approach to dealing with the Taliban of Afghanistan the best way to address the problem?"*

Examples of Ugly and their Fixes:

A survey of terrorism today.
Fix it first by narrowing to at least one arena of terrorism, then ask: *"Are acts of terror in Iraq since 2003 actually terrorism in the classic sense or a battle for power among competing factions?"*

A description of Microsoft's latest innovations.
Fix it first by narrowing to one area of operation, then ask: *"Why has Microsoft lagged so far behind Google in development of its Windows Live search engine?"*

A history of the Crusades.
Fix it first by narrowing to one aspect of the Crusades, then ask: *"Was the motivation for the first Crusade primarily religious or political/economic?"*

A1.1.4 The Fuzzy Question

Definition of Good—The question is focused clearly enough that, not only does your reader have a certainty about your goal, but so do you.

Definition of Bad—The project has a fairly narrow topic but the question is does not provide a clear mental image of your goal.

Definition of Ugly—Both the topic and its goal are not defined clearly enough to be understood.

Examples of Bad and their Fixes:

"Was it good that the once secret documents from the history of the CIA were made public?"
Fix it by pondering. Good for whom? What do you mean by "good?" Then ask, *"Was it beneficial for the ethical operation of the current CIA that the secret documents from its early days were released?"*

"What should we make of all the recent speculation about the nature and life of the historical Jesus?"
Fix it by determining what you mean by "what should we make of," then ask, *"To what extent can we say that the speculation about Jesus in the Da Vinci Code actually has merit?"*

"How can we make sense of the harm reduction policies put forward by some experts who deal with users of illegal drugs?"
Fix it by deciding what sense you want to make, then ask: *"If the harm reduction procedures for illegal drug users in Europe and Canada have been shown to reduce drug use, why are they not being implemented everywhere?"*

Examples of Ugly and their Fixes:

"Is Globalization a good thing?"
Fix it first by defining your topic. "Globalization" can be economic, political, religious, etc. Also decide what you mean by "good thing." Then ask, *"What evidence is there that the development of global free trade actually improves the economic life of the poorest producers of goods?"*

"Why are people so paranoid these days?"
Fix it by setting a definition for "paranoid." Are you speaking of a psychological condition or a mood of distrust? Next determine which people and what

they are paranoid about. Then ask, *"If serious crime rates are going down, why do so many people continue to believe that there is more crime in their neighborhoods than there once was?"*

"What's the best solution to the problem of street people?"
Fix it first by defining what you mean by "street people" (Homeless people? People who drink too much and hang around in public places? Street prostitutes? Alienated teenagers who have homes but don't want to be there?), what the problem is, and who you want to address it. Then ask, *"To what extent are volunteer organizations dealing with urban homeless people a better approach for housing them than are government sponsored programs?"*

A1.1.5 The Multi-part Question

Definition of Good—The question is absolutely singular—one goal expressed as one simple question.

Definition of Bad—There are two or more related questions on the same topic so that it is unclear which question is the primary goal.

Definition of Ugly—There are two or more questions really dealing with different aspects of the topic, so that no attempt to unify them into one question is going to succeed.

Examples of Bad and their Fixes:

"I want to look at the causes of WWI and discuss why war is a great evil and show how WWI could have been avoided."
Fix it by determining what your main goal is and eliminating any other goals or making them subordinate to the main goal. Then make it an actual question instead of an agenda statement: *In examining the causes of WWI, how could this war have been avoided? Or even: How could WWI have been avoided?* (assuming that you will have to consider the causes anyway to answer the question).

"What are the difficulties facing homeless children and how can we help further their education?"
Fix it by asking: *"Given the challenges facing homeless children, what is the best way to ensure that they get a good education?"*

"What are we doing about the use of illegal guns and how can we prevent so many young people dying in our cities?"

Fix it by asking: *What is the best way to decrease the number of shooting deaths among urban youth?*

Examples of Ugly and their Fixes:

"Will we find a cure for AIDS and how do we change public perception about it and how are we going to get the drug companies to supply cheap AIDS treatments to developing countries?"
Fix it by choosing one, then asking: *"How can we get the drug companies to supply cheap AIDS treatments to developing countries?"*

"Did Shakespeare actually write the plays attributed to him, and what are the basic features of his tragedies, and in what way could Twelfth Night *be viewed as a tragedy rather than a comedy?"*
Fix it by choosing one, then asking: *"How valid, using standard rules of interpretation, would it be to view* Twelfth Night *as a tragedy rather than a comedy?"*

"What causes Fetal Alcohol Spectrum Disorder and how can we help women not to drink during pregnancy and how could the legal system do a better job of keeping Fetal Alcohol youth and adults out of jail?"
Fix it by choosing one, then asking: *"How could the legal system do a better job of keeping Fetal Alcohol youth and adults out of jail?"*

A1.1.6 The Open-ended question

Definition of Good—The question sets its boundaries clearly so that there is no risk that the answers will go off in several different directions at once.

Definition of Bad—The question is fairly narrow, but it is capable of being answered in a variety of ways.

Definition of Ugly—The question is quite broad and is capable of being answered in a variety of ways.

Examples of Bad and their Fixes:

"What were the implications for French industry of the end of WWII?"
Fix it by determining what sorts of implications there were and narrowing a bit further. Then ask: *"What was the reason why French automobile manufacturing rebounded after WWII?"*

"What are the implications of the Crusades for modern Arabs?"

Fix it by defining "implications" more narrowly and clearly, then ask, *"What is the best way for the West to overcome the perception of some Muslims, brought on by reference to the Crusades, that it wants to destroy Islam?"*

"If we were to legalize all currently illegal drugs, what would that mean for our country?"
Fix it by defining "mean," then ask, *"How valid is the argument that legalizing all currently illegal drugs would cut crime and stabilize or diminish drug use?"*

Examples of Ugly and their Fixes:

"What trends should we be looking for in the computer world over the next decade?"
Fix it by asking narrowing dramatically, then asking: *"Will converging technologies over the next decade create a single communication device that will fulfill all the tasks done by current consumer computing and electronic interaction?"*

"What were the results of the Asian financial crisis of the 1990s?"
Fix by narrowing dramatically, then asking: *"Have Asian stock markets changed their procedures sufficiently to avoid another major crisis such as that experienced in the 1990s?"*

What does the rise of the Internet mean for information today?
Fix by narrowing dramatically, then asking: *"Why does a user created reference resource like Wikipedia succeed in providing mainly reliable information despite its lack of traditional editors?"*

A1.1.7 The Question that Will Not Fly

There is no cure for questions that simply cannot be answered given our current state of knowledge. Abandon them or foolishly devote your life to searching for solutions to things that can't be solved. Ultimately, you'll end up a delightful eccentric, but your efforts won't even raise a blip on the importance scale.

A1.1.8 Thesis Statements

Some professors prefer you to use thesis statements. Put quite simply, a thesis statement is a proposed answer to a research question. It is not a conclusion as such (which demands that you've gone through all the evidence) but a proposal, like a hypothesis in a scientific experiment, that needs to be demonstrated.

For example, you might ask: "*Are government sponsored programs or non-profit charitable programs better able to address the needs of homeless people in city cores?*" The corresponding thesis statement might be: "*Non-profit charitable programs are better able than government sponsored programs to address the needs of homeless people in city cores.*" This is not a dogmatic statement but a position you want to try to defend with evidence.

If you're not comfortable with doing research papers, the research question approach is best, because with a thesis statement there is always a tendency to prefer the evidence that supports your thesis and ignore or misuse the evidence that doesn't.

If you do take the thesis method, e.g., "The following paper will argue that ..." you need to be very careful to look at the counter-arguments as well. You might in the end be shown to be wrong.

A1.2 Practice with Research Questions

The Questions:

Determine whether or not each of the following the research questions is a good one. Then check the key below to see what I thought of the question:

1. *Did Martin Luther, the German reformer, write anything criticizing the Jews?*
2. *What effect does homelessness have on the price of beds in Canada?*
3. *What's happening with Bill Gates now that he's made all that money?*
4. *Is there evidence that changes in emphasis in the _____ Child Welfare Program in the past 5 years are the result of pressure from the press?*
5. *What happened in Iraq in 2003?*
6. *How could the looting of the museums in Iraq in 2003 have been avoided?*
7. *What are the main features of Fetal Alcohol Spectrum Disorder and what can be done both to treat and prevent this condition? Should all alcohol containers carry a warning?*
8. *What are the ethical implications of human cloning?*

Suggested Key for the Questions:

1. *Did Martin Luther, the German reformer, write anything criticizing the Jews?*

Bad Question: Anyone with the works of Luther available can find the answer in less than half an hour. Thus the arrow is already in the target. A research question is more than discovery of a fact. It has to deal with an issue that can be analyzed in depth. If it's already answered easily, the level of analysis drops to zero.

2.   *What effect does homelessness have on the price of beds in Canada?*
Bad Question: This question is the never-will-fly variety. Even if there is some connection between homelessness and the price of beds, there is no conceivable way for you to find out the nature and extent of the connection. Sometimes two ideas simply have no obvious relationship or the relationship is such that no amount of searching will help you find out what it is. A similar sort of question might be one like this: *What has been the influence of the rise of the automobile on morality in the United States?* There may be an influence, but I can think of no survey or statistical tool that would give you an answer. The key to avoiding these kinds of questions is to ask yourself: "Is there a reasonable hope that I can gather evidence that will lead to an answer?" If there seems to be no hope, drop the question.

3.   *What's happening with Bill Gates now that he's made all that money?*
Bad Question: The point is fuzzy, not focused at all. What are you trying to discover? What Bill Gates does with his day? Whether he's enjoying his money? Whether his financial give-away plan is the best use of his money? As long as your question doesn't indicate a point or a direction you have no idea how to develop your paper. Here's a good focused research question to replace it: *Is Bill Gates' plan to give away a large portion of his wealth sufficiently well organized to ensure that the money goes to the right causes?*

4.   *Is there evidence that changes in emphasis in the _____ Child Welfare Program in the past 5 years are the result of pressure from the press?*
Good Question: Why? It demands research and analysis and there is evidence available to support that research. You would need to discover when various complaints about the Ministry were prominent in the press, then see whether or not changes in the Ministry consistently followed periods of complaint.

5.   *What happened in Iraq in 2003?*
Bad Question: This question likely wants the writer to recount the story of the Iraq War (which would only be a descriptive paper), but it's not clear from the question what the author is seeking. Many things happened in Iraq in 2003.

6. *How could the looting of the museums in Iraq in 2003 have been avoided?*
Good Question: In hindsight, it should be possible to look at what happened and show what protections could have been devised to prevent the looting. Considerable writing has been done on the issue, so there should be lots of information.

7. *What are the main features of Fetal Alcohol Spectrum Disorder and what can be done both to treat and prevent this condition? Should all alcohol containers carry a warning?*
Bad Question: This is your classic multi-pointer. With this many questions to answer, you will find that your project is cut up into a number of smaller projects and has no overall unity. Follow this rule—every research project must deal with only one issue expressed by one question.

8. *What are the ethical implications of human cloning?*
Somewhat Good Question: There's a lot to research and analyze but you may well find that the question is too open-ended, so that you run into far too many ethical implications to deal with. To solve this, limit your scope. For example, ask something like this: *How does human cloning alter our definition of a 'human being'?*

A1.3 Types of Research Papers

Here are some common research paper types:

A1.3.1 Descriptive Paper

This type of essay aims at merely discovering and sharing information about something. It is not a true research paper but just a report on what you've read. Avoid this approach unless your professor explicitly asks for a reading report or survey without evaluation.

A1.3.2 Analytical or Investigative Paper

This type of essay seeks to find out the truth about something. It often focuses on questions like: Who? What? When? Where? Why? How? For example:

> ➢ *Why is the United Nations Organization so slow in responding to situations of genocide in the world?*

> ➢ *When did the Reformation actually begin?*

> ➢ *What is the truth behind the legend of Robin Hood?*

> ➢ *How were the pyramids of Egypt constructed in a time when machinery was so simple?*

A1.3.3 Persuasive Paper

This type of essay takes a position on a particular issue, seeking to persuade the reader of the truth of something and is generally expressed through a thesis statement rather than a research question. There are two major types:

> ➢ Cause and Effect—this has the goal of persuading you that something or someone was the cause or might be the cause of some event or situation. For example, consider these possible thesis statements:

> *Support for abortion creates a slippery slope in which society loses its respect for life and other policies like euthanasia are allowed to flourish.*

> *The reason why terrorism flourishes is that we have not paid sufficient attention to the problems of injustice in the world.*

> Note that cause and effect issues are notoriously difficult to demonstrate, because two events are often related only by coincidence or there are several factors at play rather than only one. To show cause and effect, you have to demonstrate that the effect was caused by one factor out of all other possible factors. That's not easy to do.

> ➢ Evaluation—this seeks to persuade you that one view is better than another on a certain topic. For example:

> *The problem of homelessness is best solved by local non-governmental initiatives rather than federal programs.*

> *Assisted suicide should be condemned, not supported, as a means to deal with the suffering of the dying.*

A1.4 The Outline as a Research Paper Guidance System

Most unsuccessful research papers have one of two problems—lack of a good, well-focused research question and/or lack of a proper structure that can take you from question to conclusion clearly and faithfully. In a research paper, this second function is done with the outline.

A1.4.1 Why worry about an outline early in the research process?

Many paper writers leave the outline to the end of the process. Some even write the paper then discern an outline so that it can be included on a contents page. The real point at which outline construction needs to begin is *once you have a research question.*

➤ The points of your outline tell you what you need to cover and thus serve as a blueprint for your research. Your outline also keeps you from missing anything.

➤ The outline gives body to your research question, showing the direction you have to take to reach your target. As you are doing your research, you will begin visualizing the completed product, thus giving your paper more depth and substance.

➤ It takes time for a paper to germinate in your thinking. The outline gives you a structure to allow that germination to develop properly.

➤ The very structure of a research paper is crucial to making the paper work. If you get things out of order, or if the order is not clear, it won't matter how much good information is there—the reader will see the paper as a failure. Thus, if you start thinking about structure and order early in the process, you are more likely to have the order right when you're done.

A1.4.2 Steps to a Good Outline

Use Your Research Question

Your research question expresses the goal of your essay. Embodied in it is the basic embryo of your outline. Here's how to turn a research question into an outline:

First, have a good look at your question and ask yourself, "What am I trying to accomplish?" In a few sentences, analyze your purpose, fleshing out your research question. Suppose your research question was:

Was the assassination of the Archduke Ferdinand as crucial a cause of WWI as is often asserted?

You could expand on it like this: There is a common view that the assassination of the Archduke created WWI. If that is true, then other circumstances will be much less significant so that the assassination pretty much single-handedly brought about the war. But if the assassination by itself was only one causal element, then the assassination may have been a final flashpoint in a more complicated process. What was that process?

Can you see how the question is leading to development of a structure?

Determine the scope of your paper

With your analysis of your research question before you, ask yourself: *What do I need to cover in order to answer my question?* Look at the example above. You will need to:

> ➢ Present and critique the common view that the assassination led to WWI

> ➢ Explain the events of that assassination and the reaction of the nations to it.

> ➢ Discover any possible larger issues of which the assassination was the final step.

> ➢ Consider all the evidence and come up with an answer to the research question.

You now have the elements of an outline. It may not be in the right order, and you may have to revise it, even add or subtract elements, but the basics are there.

Begin thinking about order

You don't need to make any final decisions about order yet, but these are some tips:

You will need an introduction that serves two purposes: to provide your reader with enough background information to be able to deal with your topic, and to declare your research question. Alternatively, you may want to formulate a thesis statement, which is a proposed answer to your question, along the lines of, "The following paper will argue that ..."

If there is any further development of background material that's more complex, it will have to go next as a separate section.

Often you will find that you are dealing with more than one point of view. Once you determine which point of view you are going to support, cover the view you do not support first, then cover the view you do support. Never reverse this order.

Think about your reader. What needs to be covered before something else makes sense? Avoid stringing out your outline into 6, 7 or more points. A structure of 3 to 5 points works far better for the reader. You should group things together so that you use fewer points, even if it means that each point has two or more sub-points.

Germinate

Memorize the outline you've created, even if it's still quite basic, and develop the habit of *germination*. What's "germination?" This is a hard thing to describe, but it's something like letting a seed grow inside of you. Take time through your day to think about your outline: *Would this order work better than that order? Have you left anything out? Have you included anything that really isn't relevant to your research question?*

Then, as you gather your books, articles, and so on, and start to read them, begin to write your paper in your head, thinking constantly about your reader: *At what points might your reader become confused? What would you change to make those points clearer? Are you being fair and complete by including all sides of an issue? Is your research question itself in need of some revision, and, if so, how will that change your outline?*

By the time you write your paper, your outline should be working well for you, and your paper should pretty much be already be written in your head.

Why do you need germination? Because depth and maturity in a research paper comes through working on it over time. Without this process, you simply have another one of those projects that are dashed off superficially and lack substance. Truly great writing needs germination. Your paper has to live and grow in you, or it will never have the power it should have for a reader. The way you allow it to grow is to build it around your ever-maturing outline.

If you have problems with leaving research projects to the last minute, you might want to start using the Assignment Calculator (**http://www.lib.umn. edu/help/freecalc/**). Its strategic approach to scheduling research papers for you is very close to the research model used in this book.

Structure your final outline

Ultimately, just when you were beginning to enjoy framing your arguments in your head, your germination process needs to come to an end. This happens somewhere either just before the writing process begins, or during the writing. But one thing needs to be complete before writing begins: your final outline, which becomes a roadmap for the final composition of your research paper, telling you at each point what you need to cover to develop your paper from introduction to conclusion. A paper written without an outline firmly before you or in your mind is a paper destined to confuse your reader and resist your hopes to communicate what you have discovered.

I cannot stress this strongly enough—your outline is the crucial element in hitting the target at which your well-formulated question is aiming.

So how do you go about structuring your final outline? If you have any uncertainty about your skills, follow a simple formula: Introduction, 3 or 4 points, Conclusion.

KEEP IT SIMPLE. If you find there is need for some complex discussion in point 2, then use sub points, like this:

Introduction
I. The events of August 1914
    A. Early Part of the Month
    B. Assassination of the Archduke
        1. The plot
        2. The perpetrator
II. The common argument that the assassination started WWI
III. A reassessment of the cause of WWI
    A.
    B.
Conclusion

A1.4.3 Practice with Outlines

For the following questions, create a 3 or 4 point outline, then compare your outline with mine in the suggested key (remember that outlines may vary):

1. *To what can we attribute the fact that Martin Luther's attitude toward Jews grew more and more negative through his lifetime?*
2. *What is the best approach to reducing homelessness in an urban setting?*
3. *Is the virtual monopoly of Microsoft really as bad for the computing world as many critics say it is?*
4. *Is there evidence that changes in emphasis in the _____ Child Welfare Program in the past 5 years are the result of pressure from the press?*
5. *How could the looting of the museums in Iraq in 2003 have been avoided?*
6. *What is the best way to deal with non-violent teens in trouble with the law but afflicted with Fetal Alcohol Spectrum Disorder (FASD)?*
7. *What are the implications of human cloning for our definition of a "person?"*
8. *Was the religious "conversion" of Roman Emperor Constantine genuine or a fraud carried out for political reasons?*

A1.4.4 Suggested Key for Practice with Outlines

1. *To what can we attribute the fact that Martin Luther's attitude toward Jews grew more and more negative through his lifetime?*

Possible Outline:
Introduction [Explain who Luther was and ask the research question]
I. Evidence of Luther's Growing Anti-Semitism
II. Possible Explanations
    A.
    B.
    C., etc.
Conclusion

2. *What is the best approach to reducing homelessness in an urban setting?*

Possible Outline:
Introduction [Explain the problem of urban homelessness and ask the research question]
I. Current Approaches to Reducing Urban Homelessness.

A.
B.
C., etc.
II. Critique of Such Approaches
    A.
    B.
    C.
III. A Proposed Best Approach
Conclusion

3. *Is the virtual monopoly of Microsoft really as bad for the computing world as many critics say it is?*

Possible Outline:
Introduction [Introduce the current monopoly issue and ask research question]
I. Arguments that the Monopoly is Bad for the Computing World
II. Arguments that the Monopoly is Good for the Computing World
Conclusion
[This outline, by putting "Good" last, assumes you are going to argue that the monopoly is good for the computing world.]

4. *Is there evidence that changes in emphasis in the _____ Child Welfare Program in the past 5 years are the result of pressure from the press?*

Possible Outline:
Introduction [Introduce the issue and ask the research question]
I. The Nature of Changes in the Program over the Past 5 Years.
II. Instances of Coordination between Press Pressure and Changes
    A. Incident One
    B. Incident Two
    C. Incident Three, etc.
III. Possible Alternate Explanations for Timing of Changes
Conclusion

5. *How could the looting of the museums in Iraq in 2003 have been avoided?*

Possible Outline:
Introduction [Explain the problem and ask the research question]
I. An Account of the Looting and the Failure to Prevent it
II. Possible Alternate Security Measures that could have Been Introduced

A.

B.

C. etc.

Conclusion [Summarize possible alternate measures and state an overall plan that might have worked better.]

6.   *What is the best way to deal with non-violent teens in trouble with the law but afflicted with Fetal Alcohol Spectrum Disorder (FASD)?*

Possible Outline:

Introduction [Explain problem of non-violent FASD offenders and ask research question]

I. Common Current Approach[es] to the Problem

II. A Critique of Such Approach[es]

III. A Suggested Better Approach

Conclusion

7.   *What are the implications of human cloning for our definition of a "person?"*

Possible Outline:

Note that this is still quite an open-ended question, allowing for several possibilities. Thus a variety of outlines are possible. Here's one.

Introduction [State the problem and ask the research question]

I. Traditional Definitions of a Person

II. Elements of Cloning that Redefine "Person."

III. A New Definition of Personhood.

Conclusion

8.   *Was the religious "conversion" of Roman Emperor Constantine genuine or a fraud carried out for political reasons?*

Possible Outline:

Introduction [Introduce Constantine and his conversion; ask the research question]

I. Evidence that the conversion was genuine.

II. Evidence that the conversion was a fraud with political motives

Conclusion

A1.5 Building the Substance of the Essay

In this section we will deal with the substance of this thing called a research essay. We will consider how it is put together and study the crucial elements that make a mature, thoughtful paper.

A1.5.1 Intent and Direction

The best research papers are characterized by strong goal-orientation. This means that they have a purpose, defined by the research question, and a sense of movement from problem to solution.

A research essay is like the flight of an arrow from bow to target. When you aim the arrow, you see a target—a specific destination. You know that to hit the target you will have a launch, a period of travel through the air, and a conclusion when the arrow hits its mark.

But an arrow in flight is also subject to things like wind speed and wind direction. Similarly, a research essay does not ignore the influencing factors—context of the issue and the various options that could be answers to the question. There needs to be opportunity for recognition and analysis of other points of view, even opposing ones, as long as you make sure you stay on target with your main intention—to answer the research question.

Here's the rule: *Every part of your paper needs to contribute ultimately to answering your research question. There is no room for irrelevant details, even if they are interesting.*

Keep your paper goal-oriented. Don't allow it to wander or lose its sense of purpose.

A1.5.2 Building the Paper

There are simple procedures that make the difference between a well-constructed paper and a mess. Here are some of them:

Use your outline like a blueprint.

Careful structure will contribute more to the success of your paper than anything else. *Follow the plan.*

You may be the sort of person who resists structure and organization in your writing, believing that structure limits your freedom of expression. But remember this: Structure is not just for your benefit, but the benefit of your reader. The reader has a distinct disadvantage. He or she does not know where you are going in your paper. Without structure, much of what you have to say will remain a mystery to the reader. With structure, your reader is never lost.

Beyond wanting to help the reader, you want to avoid leaving out anything that is important or including anything that is not important.

Carefully adhering to your outline as you write ensures that everything that needs to be in your paper is there. Write out your outline and keep it (along with your research question) ever before you as you produce your paper.

Build your paper from the paragraph up.

While sentences are the basic building blocks of communication, paragraphs are the basic building blocks of an essay. Each paragraph advances your argument, like steps in a staircase. Think of your paragraphs as the smallest sub points of each point in your outline. Each has a topic and a unity that advances whatever you are covering in the particular element of your outline.

A paragraph is a collection of sentences that develop the same theme.

Paragraphs may be as short as two sentences or as long as ten or more, but most paragraphs in a term paper will probably be between two and six sentences. If they are any longer, you should find a way to break them into smaller paragraphs.

We use paragraphs for several purposes:

➤ To introduce a new idea.

➤ To divide an idea into its parts in successive paragraphs.

➤ To give readers a break and make the essay easier to read. When I see a whole page without a paragraph break, it feels like an obstacle—too much text that needs to be read before I can take a breather. If that page is broken into paragraphs, I can pause in my reading when I want to.

➤ To help the reader to see more clearly where your thoughts are going. Every essay is like a journey through a subject. The paragraphs help the reader understand the stages of that journey.

What are the parts of a paragraph?

➢   Topic Sentence—this is usually the first sentence, though it can some-
    times be the second. This sentence tells you what the paragraph is
    about. It declares the theme or main message of the paragraph.

➢   Examples or further development intended to support the topic sen-
    tence—the sentences after the topic sentence should illustrate or sup-
    port the message of the topic sentence.

➢   Conclusion—in many paragraphs, the final sentence will give the con-
    clusion to the paragraph's idea.

When should I consider beginning a new paragraph?

➢   When you move to a new idea.

➢   When there is transition language, for example, words like "therefore,"
    "turning to the issue of _____," "on the other hand," etc.

➢   When you have just concluded an idea and the next material is illus-
    tration or further explanation.

➢   When your paragraph is getting too long. Be careful here, however,
    that you don't break for a new paragraph part way through your idea.

Some tips for paragraphs:

➢   Always check to be sure that every sentence in your paragraph sup-
    ports your topic sentence. Never have a paragraph like this:

    *There are too many people speeding on our freeways. My cousin has a
    new car, but he only drives it in town. He took me to a shopping mall the
    other day. We saw some of our friends there.*

    Notice that the sentences after the topic sentence have nothing to do
    with the topic sentence. Now look at this paragraph:

    *There are too many people speeding on our freeways. My cousin has a
    new car, but he refuses to drive it on the freeway, because he has been
    frightened by so many speeders. If we do not control the problem of speed-
    ing, a lot of people will avoid freeways, and more of those who do use
    them will die.*

➢ Make sure that each paragraph has a good relationship with the one before it and the one after it. Sometimes this means that you need to use transition words to help the reader understand where you are going, e.g., "Turning to the problem of …," "To illustrate this point, let us …," "The results of this policy, however, are …," "In conclusion …"

➢ Each paragraph must in some way support the main idea of the essay.

A1.5.3 Making Proper Use of Sources

A research paper has some very definite features that make it different from an opinion piece or a speech. First, it is an investigation of a problem, leading to a solution. This means that there is room for exhortation or application only in the conclusion, and even then the application should be brief.

Second, if a research paper is an investigation leading to a solution, it is a journey that requires the help of others, that is, the help of the books, articles, etc. that you gather during the research process. While you could simply follow a logical process of argumentation, leading to a conclusion, you need to recognize that no topic is truly original, even if your solution is different from that of most of your sources. Other thinkers have also dealt with the issue and have put forward evidence for their own interpretations.

In fact, finding a solution to a research question most often involves weighing the conflicting interpretations of others and finding your answer as a result of your evaluation.

Using sources can be tricky. At one extreme, your paper could be primarily a set of quotations from books and articles, with brief commentary from you. At the other extreme, you virtually could ignore your sources and do most of the analysis yourself. The ideal is somewhere in between, where you use your sources extensively but still keep control over the analysis.

How do you achieve the ideal use of sources?

Group your sources by the particular issues they address, and especially by the particular viewpoints they support. Thus you should have a group of sources that deal with or support view A., a group that deal with or support view B., and so on.

Keep your quotations to a minimum, usually only one quotation for every page or two. Keep the quotations under 5 lines for the most part. Instead of quoting, refer. Use language like: *Smith has argued that Constantine embraced Christianity solely because he saw its power as a political force in the Roman*

Empire. You are not quoting. You are referring to or describing a viewpoint in your own words. You'll still need to provide a citation (either in the text (Smith, 234) or as a footnote or endnote), but you'll avoid having your sources do all your speaking for you.

Recognize that the research paper is not supposed to be simply an account of what the world already knows but an analytical investigation of a problem in dialogue with others who are also addressing the problem. Thus, your own analysis, indeed your own presence, has to be seen in the paper. This means that you control your sources. They do not control you. It is you who must lay out the information that your sources provide, e.g., *Smith has argued that ... Jones provides a contrary view ... Green has added a new voice to the issue by asserting that* [and so on]. You are using your sources to be sure, but you are controlling the process.

Almost never provide new information with a quotation. Use quotations to support a statement you have made first or to present a striking way in which an author has made a point.

Use sources that you agree with as well as sources you disagree with. A research paper needs to show evidence that you've investigated all relevant points of view and have treated your sources fairly. In general, even for writers with whom you disagree, explain what the source is saying before criticizing. Let your source be heard fairly before you evaluate it. Even when you do criticize, avoid language of ridicule. Make your criticisms logical and fair.

A1.5.4 Avoiding Theft of Other People's Work

Plagiarism is passing on the thoughts or words of someone else as if they were your own. It ranges from quoting others without acknowledging them to using other people's unique ideas as if they were your unique ideas.

It's relatively easy to avoid quoting a source without using quotation marks and a bibliographical note. It's a little trickier, however, to determine if you've stolen someone's ideas. A general rule of thumb is that, if an idea is found in two or three other sources which are not all dependent on one earlier source, you can safely use it without acknowledging its source. To be on the safe side, make a bibliographical note if a source is stating a point of view rather than just well known information.

There is another source of theft that is often not recognized—the use of paraphrases by which you take your source, sentence by sentence and simply rewrite each sentence using different words. In this case, you are not interpreting and explaining your source, but using your source's paragraph structure and thoughts in something that is very close to quoting. This too is plagiarism.

Here's an excerpt from an article that I published on the Internet on the significance of electronic documents. The original paragraph is:

Thus an electronic document disrupts the very meaning of the word "document." Electronically, a "document" can be viewed from anywhere in the world at the same time via the Internet, can have its wording and its look changed at will without any sign left behind that there was an earlier version, and can encompass other documents as well as encourage reading out of order. This may seem exciting (for example, we can hyperlink a document so that any possible problem or interest a reader may experience can be answered with the click of a mouse) but it carries dangers as well. ("Electronic Documents are Different," http://www.acts.twu.ca/lbr/electronicdocs.htm).

A paraphrase, which would *not* be acceptable, might read:

Therefore an electronic document upsets the actual meaning of the word "document." In electronic form, a "document" can be seen all over the world all at once via the Internet, can have its words and what it looks like altered at will without having left behind any indication that there was an earlier form, and can include other documents as well as support the idea of reading out of order. This might seem good, but it carries dangers as well.

Notice that I've borrowed sentence structure and even words from the original without really interpreting it. Now let me express the material in my own words:

Badke argues that electronic documents are radically different from other things called "document." Electronic documents can instantly be seen everywhere on the Internet, people can alter them so that we have no idea what the original was, they can be linked to other electronic documents, and the order in which you read them may not be important.

What I have done is to *interpret* what I've read and to express it mostly in different words (though it's all right to use a few words from your source, maybe 5% or less). Remember, though, that the point of a research essay is not simply to quote or interpret others, but to evaluate their work and provide your own arguments. Your analysis is extremely important.

A1.5.5 Practice with Essay Structure

Let's walk through the development of a research paper around the following question:

Is there evidence that changes in emphasis in the _____ Child Welfare Program in the past 5 years are the result of pressure from the press?

Introduction [Introduce the issue and ask the research question]
I. The Nature of Changes in the Program over the Past 5 Years.
II. Instances of Coordination between Press Pressure and Changes
    A. Incident One
    B. Incident Two
    C. Incident Three, etc.
III. Possible Alternate Explanations for Timing of Changes
Conclusion

Here's a way we could develop our ideas:

Introduction
It is common for government departments to take press criticism seriously, even to adapt programs rather than have the press influence public opinion in a negative way. There have been many changes in the _____ Child Welfare Program over the past number of years, many of them appearing to be reactions to press criticism. Is there evidence that changes in emphasis in the _____ Child Welfare Program in the past 5 years are the result of pressure from the press?

I. The Nature of Changes in the Program over the Past 5 Years
You could survey, with documentation, the major changes that have occurred, using chronological order as your organizing principle. By doing this, you are showing evidence that significant and frequent changes have been made.
II. Instances of Coordination between Press Pressure and Changes
    A. Incident One
    B. Incident Two
    C. Incident Three, etc.
Now take each instance of change and follow this kind of structure—Incident One: Prior press reaction, timing of change, determination of whether or not the change is a correction of the problem raised by the press.

III. Possible Alternate Explanations for Timing of Changes
Now provide analysis of any other possible driving motivations for the change. You have shown a correlation between press criticism and changes, but you have not demonstrated cause and effect until you've eliminated other explanations.

Conclusion
Summarize briefly what you have covered, and make a final statement either supporting or rejecting the implication of your research question.

A1.6 Bibliographic Style

Many faculty members place an emphasis upon papers being presented in a certain style. This has long been an issue with students, both because perfect style is so hard to achieve, and because it doesn't make much sense to give so much effort to something that really doesn't seem important to the construction of a research paper. Style is important, however, for several reasons:

> ➤ The reader has fewer distractions away from content when the style (even proper title pages and tables of contents) is consistent and clear.

> ➤ The reader is better able to navigate a properly formatted paper.

> ➤ Adhering to style helps to guarantee that nothing important in the paper will be left out. This is particularly true in notes and bibliographies, where sloppy style can result in dates, volume numbers, pages, and publisher information being left out.

> ➤ Your professor wants proper style, and that makes style important in its own right (if, indeed, you're at all interested in getting good grades).

A1.6.1 Style Software

The use of bibliographic managers like RefWorks, EndNote or Zotero (see Chapter 7) has made formatting notes and bibliography much less of a painful experience than it used to be. Personally, I think students are often made to devote too much effort to getting the right punctuation in the right place in a bibliography. Most of your essay-writing effort should be focused on actually writing and revising the essay. But style is important, so what are you to do?

My recommendation is to use the electronic style resources available to you to get the grunt work done. Then, armed with a crib sheet of style examples, clean up what the software could not.

There are several types of electronic style resource available to you:

Bibliographic Managers—See Chapter 7. Most of these do not actually format your paper for you, just the notes and bibliographies (though EndNote has downloadable Word templates at **http://www.endnote.com/support/entemplates.asp**).

Commercial Style Software—Commercial style software is available for a price. It enables you to format the whole research paper, not just notes and bibliography. Let's look at what a couple of these products can do, with the disclaimer that I have received no promotional fee from these products:

EazyPaper (**http://www.eazypaper.com/index.cfm**) is a truly amazing research paper formatting program for APA, MLA and Turabian, written by one of my former students, Michael Hu, a computer genius in his own right. Not only does it enable you to format papers, notes and bibliographies, but the formatting can be configured according to your professor's specifications. It will let you input references into a database, ready to be cited in your paper (though you can't direct download or import citations from journal databases). But what about all those references you stored in RefWorks? How would you get them into EazyPaper? Easily. Just generate a bibliography of them, copy citations and paste them into the EazyPaper database. It will recognize the difference between an author and a title, etc. and generate records that you can then use for citations. In its Pro version, EazyPaper even allows you to search and download book records from a wide variety of libraries. Nice work, Michael.

StyleEase (**http://www.styleease.com/**) is a more basic program that helps you format your paper and notes/references. It allows you to compile a database of citations, though you have to enter the reference information box by box (author, title, etc.) rather than being able simply to paste a citation into the database. This is a reliable product for APA, MLA and Turabian formats.

Free Internet-based Citation Format Tools

If you lack access to a bibliographic manager and don't want to spring for style software, there are tools that can help you. By searching on the WWW for a style type with the word "template" (e.g., Turabian template, APA template), you can often find word processor templates that will help you format title pages, proper spacing, and so on. But be careful—some of these are generated by professors who have their own idiosyncratic rules for research paper style.

Professors, being the truly odd bunch that they are, may have you doing some very strange things. Or, if you're skilful, you can create your own template.

There are also citation-generating tools available. Some journal database vendors (such as EBSCO and InfoTrac) have provided the ability to save or e-mail journal records in a variety of formats. The multi-catalog search tool WorldCat (**http://www.worldcat.org**) enables you to cite any book you find in a variety of formats (open a book record and click on "Cite this Item.").

There are a couple of good citation generators online: Citation Machine (**http://www.citationmachine.net/**) and KnightCite (**http://www.calvin.edu/library/knightcite/**). Each of these asks you to choose format, type of source, then allow you to enter citation information and generate an accurate citation.

A1.6.2 Crib Sheets

All of the major bibliographic styles have their own books which detail all aspects of formatting. If you are doing serious research, buy the book.

There are, however, a number of WWW-based crib sheets that give you examples of the most common formats. These can be very useful in conjunction with bibliographic managers or style software, just to check your results (especially important with bibliographic software).

Here are some web addresses, but recognize that URLs go out of date almost as quickly as pop singers:

APA:

http://www.wooster.edu/psychology/apa-crib.html
http://www.wisc.edu/writing/Handbook/DocAPA.html
http://linguistics.byu.edu/faculty/henrichsenl/apa/apa01.html

MLA:

http://www.ccc.commnet.edu/mla/index.shtml
http://owl.english.purdue.edu/owl/resource/560/01/
http://kclibrary.nhmccd.edu/mlastyle.htm

Turabian:

http://www.bridgew.edu/Library/turabian.cfm
http://www.lib.ohio-state.edu/sites/guides/turabiangd.php
http://www.wisc.edu/writing/Handbook/DocChicago.html

Several Formats plus Sample Essays in Each Format:

http://www.dianahacker.com/resdoc/ —a terrific site for format issues! (Note: "Humanities" = MLA, "Social Sciences" = APA, "History" = Turabian, "Sciences" = CSE). Includes sample papers in all four formats.

For Electronic Items in your Bibliography—all 3 Formats Above:
http://owl.english.purdue.edu/handouts/research/r_docelectric.html

A1.7 Conclusion

Research papers do not have to be the painful experience many people make them out to be. There are some significant skills for making the writing process much easier than you think. We've seen a detailed explanation of them above, but let me summarize:

➢ Develop a well-focused analytical research question

➢ Structure your paper with a solid outline that answers the question

➢ Write intentionally, filling in the blanks in your outline with paragraphs that focus on your single goal, which is answering the research question.

➢ Use your sources skillfully and ethically at all times.

➢ Let the tools available for formatting help you produce papers that professors will find a pleasure just to look at.

Happy Researching!

APPENDIX TWO—
This Textbook and Information Literacy Competency Standards for Higher Education (ACRL)

Research Strategies conforms to the Association of College and Research Libraries, "Information Literacy Competency Standards for Higher Education." ["Information Literacy Competency Standards for Higher Education." American Library Association. 2006. http://www.ala.org/acrl/ilcomstan.html (Accessed 3 December, 2007). Used by permission.]

For a comparative index showing which portions of Research Strategies (3rd ed., 2008) are relevant to the various ACRL standards, go to: http://www.acts.twu.ca/lbr/resACRL.htm

APPENDIX THREE—
Second and Third Edition, a
Comparative Table

For a table comparing tables of contents of the second edition (2004) and third edition (2008) of *Research Strategies*, go to: **http://www.acts.twu.ca/lbr/comparison.htm**

Index

978-0-595-47747-0
0-595-47747-X

Printed in the United States
125402LV00004B/205/P